Copyright © 2016 Time Inc. Books

Published by Time Inc. Books
225 Liberty Street
New York, NY 10281

FOOD & WINE is a trademark of Time Inc.
Affluent Media Group, registered in the
U.S. and other countries.

ISBN 10: 0-8487-4842-5
ISBN 13: 978-0-8487-4842-5

Library of Congress Number: 2016948387

Printed in the United States of America
10 9 8 7 6 5 4 3 2 1
First Edition 2016

EXECUTIVE EDITOR **Kate Heddings**
EDITOR **Susan Choung**
DESIGNER **Alisha Petro**
COPY EDITOR **Lisa Leventer**
EDITORIAL ASSISTANT **Taylor Rondestvedt**
PRODUCTION DIRECTOR **Joseph Colucci**
PRODUCTION MANAGER **Stephanie Thompson**

PRINCIPAL PHOTOGRAPHY (INCLUDING COVERS)
PHOTOGRAPHER **John Kernick**
FOOD STYLIST **Hadas Smirnoff**
PROP STYLIST **Marie Sullivan**
For additional photo contributors,
see page 255.

ILLUSTRATIONS **Andrew Gibbs (icons),
Chris Philpot (how-tos)**

FOOD & WINE
EDITOR **Nilou Motamed**
CREATIVE DIRECTOR **Fredrika Stjärne**
EXECUTIVE EDITOR **Pamela Kaufman**
ART DIRECTOR **James Maikowski**
PHOTO EDITOR **Sara Parks**
PHOTO ASSISTANT **Rebecca Delman**

MAD GENIUS TIPS

Over 90 Expert Hacks + 100 Delicious Recipes

By Justin Chapple
and the Editors of FOOD & WINE

FOOD & WINE
BOOKS

CONTENTS

FOREWORD

Justin Chapple is FOOD & WINE's resident ham: He's constantly singing show tunes, cracking jokes or playing pranks on unsuspecting co-workers in our New York City Test Kitchen. But we all gladly put up with it, not just because Justin's so charming and funny but also because he's got serious cooking chops and a huge imagination.

All of this explains why his Mad Genius Tips videos and recipes, showcasing brilliant and unexpected ways to hack basic kitchen tools, have become such a phenomenon. Who knew that a crosshatch baking rack could quickly dice avocados? That a Bundt pan could double as a rotisserie for chicken? That a 12-cup muffin tin could poach a dozen eggs at once?

In this book, you'll discover more than 90 brilliant tricks to make over 100 incredible dishes, each rigorously conceived and tested. So you're guaranteed the foolproof recipes you expect from FOOD & WINE, injected with a healthy dose of fun.

You'll be happy to eat any of the wonderful dishes in this book, and the energy and creativity that Justin brings to every hack will keep you turning the pages. For even more ideas–and to see Justin in action–check out his Mad Genius Tips videos at foodandwine.com.

Nilou Motamed
Editor
FOOD & WINE

Kate Heddings
Executive Editor
FOOD & WINE Cookbooks

ALUMINUM FOIL

BAKE HEART-SHAPED CUPCAKES

Who needs a heart-shaped muffin pan? I make little balls of aluminum foil, which push in the batter to create adorable shapes.

STEP 1 Line the cups of a muffin tin with foil liners. Scoop cupcake batter into each cup.

STEP 2 Roll foil into marble-size balls. Gently pull back the liner of each filled cupcake and drop a foil ball between the liner and the pan.

Heart-Shaped Coconut Cupcakes

Active **30 min;** Total **1 hr 20 min**
Makes **2 dozen**

CUPCAKES

- 2 cups all-purpose flour
- 1¼ tsp. baking powder
- ½ tsp. kosher salt
- 1½ sticks unsalted butter, softened
- 1½ cups granulated sugar
- 3 large eggs
- ¼ cup coconut oil, melted and cooled slightly
- 1½ tsp. pure vanilla extract
- ¾ cup whole milk
- 2 cups sweetened shredded coconut

FROSTING

- 1 cup heavy cream
- ¼ cup confectioners' sugar
- ½ tsp. pure coconut extract

1. Make the cupcakes Preheat the oven to 350° and line the cups of two 12-cup muffin tins with foil liners. Tear a large sheet of aluminum foil into 24 pieces, then roll them into balls that are approximately the size of marbles.

2. In a medium bowl, whisk the flour with the baking powder and salt. In a large bowl, using a hand mixer, beat the butter with the granulated sugar at medium-high speed until fluffy. Beat in the eggs one at a time, then beat in the coconut oil and vanilla. At low speed, beat in the milk and the dry ingredients in alternating batches. Fold in the shredded coconut. Scoop the batter into the lined muffin cups. Place a foil ball between each cupcake liner and the pan.

3. Bake the cupcakes in the upper and lower thirds of the oven for 17 to 20 minutes, until springy and a toothpick inserted in the center of a cupcake comes out clean; shift the pans from top to bottom and front to back halfway through baking. Let the cupcakes cool slightly in the pan, then transfer them to a rack to cool completely; discard the foil balls.

4. Make the frosting In a bowl, using a hand mixer, beat the cream with the confectioners' sugar and coconut extract until stiff. Frost the cupcakes and serve.

DIY YOUR STEAMER

Steaming food is not only healthy, it maximizes juiciness–especially in something like fish, which can dry out easily. But if you don't have a bamboo steamer, I have the ultimate tip for creating a makeshift one. All you need is some aluminum foil and a deep skillet.

 Place three balls of aluminum foil in a large, deep skillet. Set a heatproof plate of food on top of the foil balls, add water to the skillet and cover to steam.

Steamed Black Bass with Crispy Garlic
Total **40 min**; Serves **4**

    Canola oil, for frying

 3 large garlic cloves, very thinly
    sliced

    Kosher salt and pepper

    Four 5-oz. black sea bass fillets,
    with skin

1½ Tbsp. fresh lime juice

 1 Tbsp. Asian fish sauce

 1 Tbsp. minced scallion, plus 1 thinly
    sliced scallion for garnish

 2 tsp. minced peeled fresh ginger

 1 cup cilantro leaves

    Lime wedges, for serving

1. In a small skillet, heat ¼ inch of oil over moderate heat. Add the garlic and cook over moderately low heat, stirring, until golden and crisp, 5 minutes. Using a slotted spoon, transfer to a paper towel–lined plate to drain. Season with salt.

2. With a paring knife, make 3 or 4 shallow slashes in the skin of each fish fillet. In a small bowl, mix the lime juice with the fish sauce, minced scallion and ginger. Rub the mixture on both sides of the fish and into the slashes. Season the fillets lightly with salt and pepper and place them skin side up on a large heatproof plate that will fit in your skillet.

3. Make a steamer by arranging 3 balls (a little smaller than baseballs) of foil in a large, deep skillet. Set the plate with the fish on top of the balls. Add 1 inch of water to the skillet and bring to a boil. Cover the skillet and steam the fish over moderately high heat until white throughout, 5 to 7 minutes. Using a spatula, transfer the fillets to a platter and spoon the juices on top. Pile the cilantro and sliced scallion on the fillets, sprinkle the crispy garlic on top and serve with lime wedges.

4 more ways to use your DIY steamer

DUMPLINGS Place fresh or frozen dumplings on a heatproof plate lined with parchment paper or lightly greased with a neutral oil like canola. Add water to the skillet, cover and steam until the dumpling filling is firm and cooked through.

SHRIMP Arrange shrimp on a heatproof plate and rub with scallion-ginger sauce (at left). Add water to the skillet, cover and steam until the shrimp are pink and slightly curled.

CHICKEN Set a chicken breast on a heatproof plate, rub with scallion-ginger sauce (at left) and season with salt. Add water to the skillet, cover and steam until an instant-read thermometer inserted in the thickest part of the breast registers 160°.

VEGETABLES Spread out your vegetables on a heatproof plate (broccoli, cauliflower, asparagus, green beans and carrots are good options). Add water to the skillet, cover and steam until crisp-tender.

CREATE A BAKING RACK FOR BACON

 Fold the edge of a double layer of aluminum foil. Flip the foil and fold the edge again. Continue flipping and folding the foil accordion-style to form a disposable baking rack.

Candied Bacon with Aleppo

Active **10 min**; Total **40 min plus cooling**
Serves **4 to 6**

12 oz. thick-cut bacon

½ cup packed light brown sugar

Aleppo pepper, for sprinkling

1. Preheat the oven to 400°. Lay a very large double layer of foil on a work surface. Starting at a short end, fold the edge of the foil to make a ½-inch-wide pleat. Flip the foil and fold the edge again. Continue to flip and fold the foil accordion-style to form a baking rack. Transfer to a large rimmed baking sheet.

2. Arrange the bacon in a single layer on the foil rack and bake until browned but not crisp, about 15 minutes. Sprinkle the bacon with the sugar, season with Aleppo pepper and bake until glazed, 15 to 20 minutes longer. Let the bacon cool on the rack until crisp before serving.

MAKE A PERFORATED GRILL PAN

My trick for replicating a perforated grill pan is going to seriously up your cookout game–especially for grilling all sorts of small ingredients that would otherwise fall through the grate: snap peas, green beans, radishes, baby potatoes–even berries.

 Lay heavy-duty aluminum foil over a baking rack. Poke holes through the foil with the tip of scissors.

Blistered Snap Peas with Burrata and Mint
Total **30 min;** Serves **4**

Grilling snap peas in a perforated grill pan gives them a smoky char all over. I cook them quickly so they stay crisp.

- 3 Tbsp. fresh lemon juice
- 1 tsp. honey
- 1 tsp. Dijon mustard
- ¼ cup plus 1 Tbsp. extra-virgin olive oil
-   Kosher salt and pepper
- 12 oz. snap peas, strings removed
- 1 cup lightly packed mint leaves
- 1 lb. burrata, cut into chunks (see Note)

1. Lay a large triple layer of heavy-duty foil over a baking rack. Using the point of a pair of scissors, poke ½-inch-wide holes through the foil, twisting the scissors to form circles.

2. Slide the foil pan onto a grill and then light the grill. In a small bowl, whisk the lemon juice with the honey and mustard. Gradually whisk in ¼ cup of the olive oil until emulsified. Season the dressing with salt and pepper.

3. In a large bowl, toss the peas with the remaining 1 tablespoon of olive oil and season with salt and pepper. Spread the peas on the perforated foil pan and grill over high heat, undisturbed, until lightly charred, about 2 minutes. Using a wooden spoon, gently stir and grill until hot, 30 seconds to 1 minute longer. Transfer the peas to a bowl and toss with the mint and half of the dressing.

4. Arrange the burrata on 4 plates. Spoon the peas on top and drizzle with the remaining dressing. Serve right away.

NOTE If you can't find burrata, you can use buffalo mozzarella.

BAKING RACK

WEAVE BACON

The BLT often misses its shot at greatness due to one flaw: There isn't bacon in every bite. Now, with the help of this tip, it wins my award for Most Amazing Sandwich. I weave uncooked strips of bacon into a tight lattice, then bake until crisp, so I get crunchy, smoky bacon throughout.

STEP 1 Cut bacon slices in half crosswise.

STEP 2 On a parchment-lined baking sheet, weave 6 strips of bacon, 3 in each direction, to create a lattice.

STEP 3 Lay a baking rack upside down on the bacon lattices to keep them flat. Bake until browned and crisp.

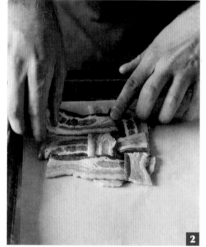

California BLTs
Total **45 min**; Serves **4**

12 slices of bacon, halved crosswise

½ cup mayonnaise

 1 Tbsp. finely chopped tarragon

 1 Tbsp. fresh lemon juice

    Kosher salt and pepper

 8 slices of multigrain sandwich bread, toasted

 1 Hass avocado—peeled, pitted and sliced

 2 Persian cucumbers, thinly sliced on the diagonal

 1 medium tomato, thinly sliced

 4 small Bibb lettuce leaves

½ cup mixed sprouts, such as radish, sunflower and alfalfa

1. Preheat the oven to 400°. Line a large rimmed baking sheet with parchment paper or foil. For each lattice, weave 6 strips of bacon, 3 in each direction, on the prepared baking sheet.

2. Set a baking rack upside down on the bacon to keep it flat. Bake for 15 to 20 minutes, until browned and crisp. Remove the rack, then transfer the bacon lattices to paper towels to drain.

3. Meanwhile, in a small bowl, whisk the mayonnaise with the tarragon and lemon juice. Season with salt and pepper.

4. Spread the tarragon mayonnaise on each slice of toast. Arrange the sliced avocado, cucumbers and tomato on 4 slices of the toast and sprinkle with salt and pepper. Top with the bacon lattices, Bibb leaves and sprouts. Close the sandwiches and serve.

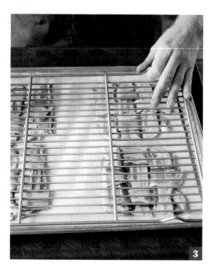

MAKE GUACAMOLE

STEP 1 Halve and pit an avocado.

STEPS 2 AND 3 Press through a crosshatch baking rack to create perfect cubes.

1

2

3

Guacamole with Charred Pineapple

Total **15 min;** Makes **2 cups**

- Two ½-inch-thick rings of fresh pineapple
- 2 large avocados, halved and pitted
- ½ cup chopped cilantro
- ¼ cup minced red onion
- 2½ Tbsp. fresh lime juice
- Kosher salt and pepper

1. Heat a large cast-iron skillet over high heat until smoking. Add the pineapple and cook over high heat, turning once, until lightly charred on both sides, 4 minutes. Let cool, then finely dice.

2. Set a crosshatch baking rack over a large bowl. Put an avocado half cut side down on the rack and, using your palm, press it through the rack until the skin remains in your hand; discard the skin. Repeat with the remaining avocado halves. Fold in the pineapple, cilantro, onion and lime juice. Season generously with salt and pepper and serve.

CHOP BOILED EGGS

I stole this egg-salad hack from chef Jamie Bissonnette of Toro in Boston. Instead of using a knife, he dices boiled eggs perfectly and quickly with a crosshatch baking rack.

STEP 1 Place an egg on a crosshatch baking rack set over a bowl.

STEP 2 Press the egg through the rack with a plate.

Chopped Egg and Baby Potato Salad

Active **30 min**; Total **1 hr**; Serves **6**

- 6 large eggs
- 1¼ lbs. baby red potatoes
  Kosher salt and pepper
- ½ cup extra-virgin olive oil
- ¼ cup Champagne vinegar
- 1 Tbsp. whole-grain mustard
- 1 small red onion, halved and thinly sliced
- 1½ cups lightly packed baby arugula
- 1 cup lightly packed parsley, chopped
- ½ cup lightly packed dill, chopped

1. In a medium saucepan, cover the eggs with water and bring to a boil. Simmer over moderate heat for 8 minutes. Drain and cool under running water, then peel.

2. In the saucepan, cover the potatoes with water and bring to a boil. Add a generous pinch of salt and simmer over moderate heat until tender, about 15 minutes. Drain well and let cool slightly.

3. In a large bowl, whisk the olive oil with the vinegar and mustard. Season with salt and pepper. Set a crosshatch baking rack over the bowl. Put 1 egg on the rack and, using a small plate, press it through the rack. Repeat with the remaining eggs and the potatoes. Add the onion, arugula, parsley and dill and gently fold to mix. Season generously with salt and pepper and fold again. Serve.

MAKE AHEAD The egg and potato salad can be refrigerated for up to 6 hours. Bring to room temperature and fold in the onion, arugula, parsley and dill before serving.

SKIN HAZELNUTS

Removing the papery husks from hazelnuts usually takes a lot of work, but my baking rack trick lets you skin a bunch at once with virtually no mess.

STEP 1 Set a crosshatch baking rack over a baking sheet. Spread hazelnuts on the rack and toast in the oven.

STEP 2 Rub the nuts on the rack so the skins peel off and fall away.

Chocolate-Hazelnut Tart

Active **50 min**; Total **2 hr 45 min**
Makes **one 9-inch tart**; Serves **10**

CRUST

- 1 **stick unsalted butter**
- 2 **Tbsp. sugar**
- ¼ **tsp. kosher salt**
- 1½ **cups graham cracker crumbs (12 to 14 whole crackers or 7 oz.)**

FILLING

- 1½ **cups hazelnuts**
- 1¼ **cups heavy cream**
- 2 **Tbsp. strong brewed coffee**
- 12 **oz. bittersweet chocolate, finely chopped**
- 2 **Tbsp. unsalted butter, softened**
- ¼ **tsp. kosher salt**

1. Make the crust In a small saucepan, melt the butter with the sugar and salt over moderately low heat, stirring, until the sugar dissolves, about 4 minutes. In a medium bowl, mix the graham cracker crumbs with the butter mixture until the crumbs are evenly moistened. Press the crumbs evenly over the bottom and up the side of a 9-inch fluted tart pan. Cover with plastic wrap and refrigerate until well chilled, about 1 hour.

2. Meanwhile, make the filling Preheat the oven to 375°. Spread the hazelnuts on a crosshatch baking rack set over a large rimmed baking sheet. Bake for about 10 minutes, until golden. Let cool. Using your palms, rub the hazelnuts against the rack to remove the skins, then coarsely chop the nuts.

3. In a medium saucepan, bring the cream and coffee just to a simmer. Add all but ¼ cup of the chopped chocolate to the saucepan along with the butter and salt. Let stand for 2 minutes, then stir until smooth. Scrape the chocolate cream into the tart shell and scatter the hazelnuts on top, lightly pressing them into the chocolate.

4. In a small microwavable bowl, heat the remaining ¼ cup of chopped chocolate at high power in 20-second intervals until melted. Drizzle the melted chocolate on the tart in decorative circles. Refrigerate until firm, about 1½ hours. Remove the tart ring, cut the tart into wedges and serve.

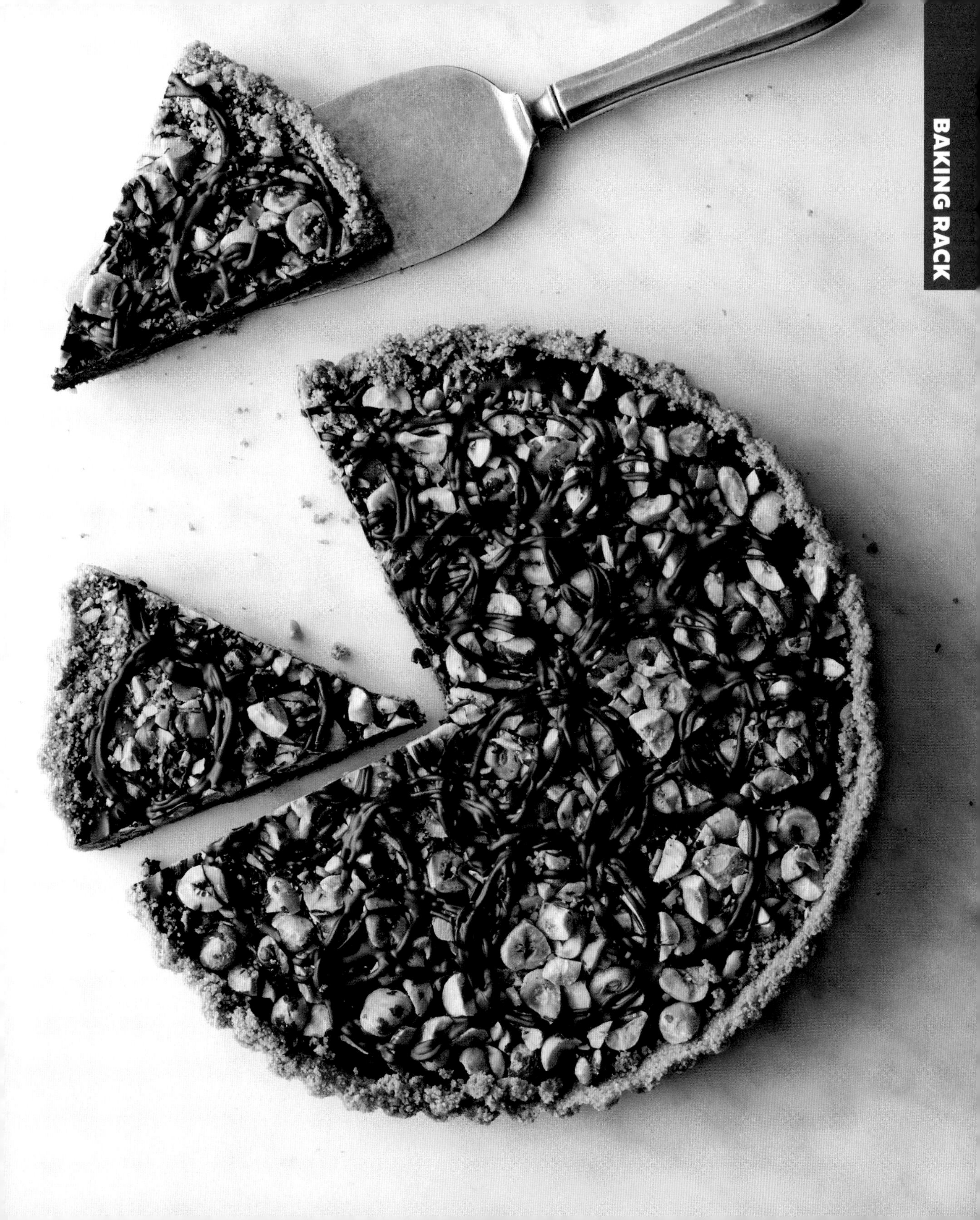

BOX GRATER

MAKE TOMATO SAUCE

Most people don't make tomato sauce at home because they're in a hurry. But my box grater trick creates fresh, flavorful tomato sauce that you don't even have to cook.

STEP 1 Rub ripe tomato halves on the large holes of a box grater until only the skin remains in your hand.

STEP 2 Stir olive oil into the grated tomato to create a fresh, no-cook tomato sauce.

Brussels Sprout and Robiola Pizza with Fresh Tomato Sauce

Active **25 min**; Total **1 hr**; Serves **4**

The mild flavor and silky texture of Robiola Bosina cheese is delicious with brussels sprouts.

- 1 **medium tomato, halved crosswise**
- 1 **Tbsp. extra-virgin olive oil, plus more for drizzling**

  Kosher salt and black pepper
- 1 **lb. pizza dough**
- 6 **oz. Robiola Bosina cheese, cut into ¼-inch-thick slices with the rind**
- 6 **oz. brussels sprouts, trimmed and very thinly sliced**
- ¼ **tsp. crushed red pepper**

1. Set a pizza stone on a rack in the bottom third of the oven. Preheat the oven to 500° for at least 30 minutes.

2. Working over a medium bowl, grate the tomato halves on the large holes of a box grater until only the skin remains in your hand; discard the skin. Stir in the 1 tablespoon of olive oil and season the sauce with salt and black pepper.

3. On a lightly floured work surface, press and stretch the dough to a 12-inch round; avoid pressing on the outermost edge. Transfer the dough to a lightly floured pizza peel. Spread the tomato sauce on the dough, leaving a 1-inch border. Top with the cheese, brussels sprouts and crushed red pepper. Season with salt and black pepper.

4. Slide the pizza onto the pizza stone. Bake until the bottom is lightly charred and the top is lightly browned, 12 to 15 minutes. Lightly drizzle the pizza with olive oil, cut into wedges and serve.

MAKE AHEAD The fresh tomato sauce can be refrigerated overnight.

SHRED FLAVORED BUTTER

I keep a secret weapon in my freezer: a log of compound (flavored) butter. I could slice it into rounds, but grating it is so much better because the little curls melt quickly and evenly. Thick cuts of meat (like the tri-tip here) especially benefit from a flavor boost all over.

 Shred frozen compound butter on the large holes of a box grater to flavor meat, poultry or seafood.

Tri-Tip Roast with Chimichurri Butter

Active **30 min**; Total **1 hr plus 2 hr freezing**; Serves **4 to 6**

- 1 **stick unsalted butter, softened**
- ¼ **cup minced parsley**
- 2 **Tbsp. minced drained capers**
- 1½ **tsp. finely grated lemon zest plus 1 Tbsp. fresh lemon juice**
- 1 **large garlic clove, minced**
- ½ **tsp. crushed red pepper**
- **Kosher salt and black pepper**
- **One 1½-lb. tri-tip roast (2 inches thick)**
- 1 **Tbsp. canola oil**

1. In a medium bowl, using a fork, blend the butter with the parsley, capers, lemon zest and juice, garlic and crushed red pepper. Season the chimichurri butter generously with salt and black pepper and scrape it onto a piece of plastic wrap.

Fold the sides over the butter and shape it into a log, twisting the ends to seal. Freeze until firm, about 2 hours.

2. Preheat the oven to 425°. Season the roast all over with salt and black pepper. In a large cast-iron skillet, heat the oil until shimmering. Add the roast and cook over moderately high heat, turning occasionally, until browned all over, about 8 minutes. Transfer the skillet to the oven and roast for 15 to 20 minutes, until an instant-read thermometer inserted in the thickest part of the meat registers 120°. Transfer the roast to a carving board, tent with foil and let rest for 10 minutes.

3. Unwrap one end of the chimichurri butter. Slice the meat against the grain and transfer to a platter. Using a box grater, shred some of the chimichurri butter over the meat and serve right away, with the remaining butter on the side.

MAKE AHEAD The chimichurri butter can be frozen for up to 1 month.

better with flavored butter

POPCORN Who doesn't love hot buttered popcorn? I make a big batch in an enameled cast-iron casserole and immediately top it with a generous grating of flavored butter. A quick toss completely coats the warm kernels.

OMELETS Omelets are great for using up odds and ends and leftovers, but sometimes I find the refrigerator drawer empty. That's where my frozen flavored butter comes to the rescue. After sliding my omelet onto a plate, I finely grate the butter on top.

BREAD I love to toast slices of crusty bread like baguette, ciabatta and sourdough and then grate flavored butter on top. It's tastier than plain butter and melts super-quickly.

PREP FRESH PASTA

Using a box grater means you can make fresh pasta without a hand-cranked machine or an electric one. I love the grated pasta in this hearty soup recipe. It's also amazing simply boiled and tossed with olive oil, or boiled and sautéed in butter like spaetzle.

STEP 1 Whisk flour with salt in a bowl.

STEP 2 Stir in egg and olive oil until a dry, shaggy dough forms.

STEP 3 Knead the dough on a work surface until smooth.

STEP 4 Shape the dough into a ball for grating.

STEP 5 Grate the dough on the large holes of a box grater.

Pork Meatballs and Grated Pasta in Brodo

Active **45 min**; Total **1 hr 15 min**
Serves **6**

PASTA

- 1 **cup all-purpose flour**
- ½ **tsp. kosher salt**
- 1 **large egg, lightly beaten**
- 1 **Tbsp. extra-virgin olive oil**

SOUP

- ½ **lb. ground pork**
- 1 **large egg, lightly beaten**
- ¼ **cup plus 2 Tbsp. panko**
- 2 **Tbsp. milk**
- 2 **Tbsp. minced parsley**
- ¼ **cup plus 2 Tbsp. freshly grated Parmigiano-Reggiano cheese**
- **Kosher salt and pepper**
- 2 **Tbsp. extra-virgin olive oil**
- 4 **medium carrots, cut into ½-inch pieces**
- 1 **medium leek, white and light green parts only, halved lengthwise and sliced ½ inch thick**
- 3 **large garlic cloves, thinly sliced**
- 2 **qts. chicken stock or low-sodium broth**
- 4 **cups curly spinach, stemmed**

1. Make the pasta In a medium bowl, whisk the flour with the salt. Stir in the egg and olive oil until a shaggy dough forms. Turn the dough out onto a work surface and knead until smooth (the dough will be slightly dry), then shape it into a ball. Using the large holes of a box grater, grate the dough onto a large baking sheet. Let stand at room temperature for 30 minutes.

2. Meanwhile, make the soup In a large bowl, combine the pork with the egg, panko, milk, parsley, 2 tablespoons of the Parmesan, 1 teaspoon of salt and ½ teaspoon of pepper and mix well. Form the mixture into 1-inch balls.

3. In a large saucepan, heat the olive oil. Add the meatballs and cook over moderate heat, turning occasionally, until lightly browned all over, about 5 minutes. Using a slotted spoon, transfer to a plate. Add the carrots, leek and garlic to the saucepan and cook, stirring, until just starting to soften, about 5 minutes. Add the stock and 1 cup of water and bring to a boil over high heat.

4. Add the meatballs to the broth and simmer over moderate heat until the meatballs are cooked through and the vegetables are just tender, about 5 minutes. Add the grated pasta and simmer until al dente, about 5 minutes. Stir in the spinach and remaining ¼ cup of Parmesan, then season with salt and pepper. Ladle the soup into shallow bowls and serve right away.

MAKE AHEAD The pasta can be prepared through Step 1 and frozen in an airtight container for up to 1 month.

DIY YOUR BREAD CRUMBS

Making bread crumbs on a box grater is the ultimate zero-waste method (think of all those bread heels in your freezer!). I also have a bonus hack within a hack: Grate the bread inside a resealable bag so the crumbs don't go flying.

 Rub lightly toasted bread on the large holes of a box grater to create instant bread crumbs.

how to use a box grater

LARGE HOLES This side of the box grater is ideal for making panko-size bread crumbs. They are delicious on the leeks here, or as a coating for shrimp tempura.

SMALL HOLES These will yield medium-size bread crumbs, which are perfect for mixing into meat loaf or meatballs.

SPIKY HOLES For the finest bread crumbs of all, use this side. It's important that the bread is dry so it's easier to grate. These crumbs, which resemble the store-bought kind, are excellent for coating cutlets before frying.

SLICING EDGE Commonly used in place of a mandoline for cutting ingredients like potatoes, it also works on thick, dense loaves like black bread. You'll end up with little shards that can be toasted in olive oil and sprinkled over soup.

Braised Leeks with Fennel Bread Crumbs

Total **45 min**; Serves **4**

  One 1-inch-thick slice of stale sourdough bread, lightly toasted

¼ cup extra-virgin olive oil

1½ tsp. ground fennel

  Kosher salt and pepper

4 leeks, white and light green parts only, halved lengthwise

½ cup chicken stock or low-sodium broth

2 large garlic cloves, thinly sliced

1 thyme sprig

  Chopped parsley, for garnish

1. Open a large, resealable plastic bag and set a box grater in it. Grate the bread into the bag on the large holes of the grater. Measure out ½ cup of the crumbs and reserve the rest for another use.

2. In a small skillet, heat 1 tablespoon of the olive oil. Add the bread crumbs and ground fennel and cook over moderately high heat, stirring, until golden and fragrant, about 3 minutes. Season with salt and pepper.

3. In a large, deep skillet, heat the remaining 3 tablespoons of olive oil. Add the leeks cut side down and cook over moderately high heat until browned on the bottom, 3 to 4 minutes. Turn the leeks over and add the chicken stock, garlic and thyme. Season with salt and pepper and bring to a boil. Cover and simmer over moderately low heat until the leeks are tender, 8 to 10 minutes. Sprinkle half of the bread crumbs on top and garnish with chopped parsley. Serve, passing the remaining bread crumbs at the table.

MAKE AHEAD The fennel bread crumbs can be stored in an airtight container for up to 1 week.

BAKE FLAKY PASTRY

A box grater is my quick cheat for cutting cold butter into flour for the flakiest pastry.

 STEP 1 Shred a frozen stick of butter on the large holes of a box grater.

STEP 2 Toss the grated butter in flour. Stir in ice water.

STEP 3 Gently knead the dough on a work surface just until it comes together. Shape the dough into a disk, wrap in plastic and refrigerate until well chilled.

Spring Vegetable Galette

Active **40 min**; Total **2 hr**; Serves **4**

DOUGH

- 1¼ cups all-purpose flour
- ¾ tsp. each of kosher salt and pepper
- 1 stick unsalted butter, frozen
- ⅓ cup ice water
- Milk, for brushing

TOPPINGS

- 3 medium carrots, thinly sliced on the diagonal
- 4 oz. baby red potatoes, very thinly sliced
- 4 oz. medium asparagus (¼ bunch), trimmed and cut into 1½-inch lengths
- 4 large scallions, cut into 1½-inch lengths
- 1½ Tbsp. extra-virgin olive oil
- ½ tsp. finely grated lemon zest
- Kosher salt and pepper
- ½ cup quark or sour cream
- 2 Tbsp. freshly grated Parmesan cheese

1. Make the dough In a large bowl, whisk the flour with the salt and pepper. Working over the bowl, grate the butter on the large holes of a box grater. Gently toss the grated butter in the flour to distribute it evenly. Stir in the ice water until evenly moistened. Scrape the dough out onto a work surface, gather up any crumbs and knead gently just until the dough comes together. Shape into a disk, wrap in plastic and refrigerate until well chilled, about 1 hour.

2. Preheat the oven to 450°. On a lightly floured work surface, roll out the dough to a 14-inch round. Slide the pastry onto a parchment paper–lined rimmed baking sheet and refrigerate for 15 minutes.

3. Prepare the toppings In a large bowl, toss the carrots, potatoes, asparagus, scallions, oil and lemon zest. Season with salt and pepper. In a small bowl, whisk the quark and Parmesan; spread on the pastry, leaving a 1½-inch border. Scatter the vegetables on the quark. Fold the pastry edge up and over the vegetables to create a 1½-inch border. Brush the edge of the pastry with milk.

4. Bake the galette for 20 to 25 minutes, until the pastry is browned and crisp and the vegetables are tender. Let cool slightly, cut into wedges and serve warm.

BUNDT
PAN

CUT CORN OFF THE COB

 Insert the bottom of a shucked ear of corn into the center pillar of a Bundt pan. Using a sharp knife, cut off the kernels, turning the ear as you go.

Corn and Barley Salad

Active **25 min;** Total **50 min;** Serves **4 to 6**

- ½ cup pearled barley
- ¾ cup walnuts
- 3 cups fresh corn kernels (from about 4 ears)
- ¾ cup chopped pitted mild green olives
- ¼ cup chopped dill
- ¼ cup snipped chives
- ¼ cup extra-virgin olive oil
- 3 Tbsp. fresh lemon juice
  Kosher salt and pepper

1. Preheat the oven to 375°. In a medium saucepan of salted boiling water, cook the barley until just tender, about 25 minutes. Drain well and spread out on a plate to cool completely.

2. Spread the walnuts in a pie plate and toast for about 12 minutes, until golden. Let cool, then coarsely chop.

3. In a large bowl, toss the barley with the corn, walnuts and all of the remaining ingredients. Season with salt and pepper and serve.

CONTINUED ▶

CUT CORN OFF THE COB

Corn-Studded Corn Muffins with Honey Mascarpone

Active **20 min**; Total **1 hr**; Makes **12**

- 1 cup all-purpose flour
- 1 cup finely ground cornmeal
- ½ cup sugar
- 1 Tbsp. baking powder
  Kosher salt
- 2 large eggs
- 1 cup buttermilk, at room temperature
- 1 stick unsalted butter, melted
- 1 cup fresh corn kernels (from about 1½ ears)
- ½ cup mascarpone cheese
- 1½ Tbsp. honey

1. Preheat the oven to 350° and line a 12-cup muffin tin with paper or foil liners. In a medium bowl, whisk the flour with the cornmeal, sugar, baking powder and 1 teaspoon of salt. In a large bowl, beat the eggs with the buttermilk and melted butter. Whisk in the dry ingredients, then fold in the corn kernels.

2. Spoon the batter into the prepared muffin cups. Bake for 15 to 18 minutes, until a toothpick inserted in the centers of the muffins comes out clean. Let the corn muffins cool in the pan for 10 minutes before turning them out onto a wire rack to cool completely.

3. In a small bowl, whisk the mascarpone with the honey and a pinch of salt. Serve with the muffins.

Whipped Corn Dip with Chili Oil

Total **30 min**; Serves **6**

- 3 Tbsp. unsalted butter
- 2 cups fresh corn kernels (from about 3 ears)
- 1 large shallot, minced
- 1 garlic clove, minced
- ½ cup fresh ricotta cheese
- 1½ Tbsp. fresh lemon juice
- Kosher salt and white pepper
- Chili oil, for garnish
- Crudités or pita chips, for serving

In a large skillet, melt the butter. Add the corn, shallot and garlic and cook over moderate heat until the corn is crisp-tender, about 7 minutes. Scrape into a food processor and let cool slightly. Add the ricotta, lemon juice and 1 tablespoon of water and puree until very smooth. Season with salt and white pepper. Transfer the dip to a bowl and drizzle with chili oil. Serve with crudités or pita chips.

MAKE AHEAD The dip can be refrigerated overnight. Serve at room temperature.

ROAST CHICKEN

Roasting chicken upright in a Bundt pan lets the bird brown all over. Plus, the juices can flavor veggies layered beneath so they won't dry out the way they do in a baking pan.

STEP 1 Cover the center pillar of a Bundt pan with foil so the chicken juices don't escape.

STEP 2 Toss sausages and vegetables with olive oil in a bowl. Season with salt and pepper. Add to the Bundt pan.

STEP 3 Perch the chicken on the pan by inserting the center pillar into the cavity.

Roast Chicken with Sausage and Peppers

📷 PAGE 50

Active **30 min;** Total **1 hr 45 min;** Serves **4**

- ¾ **lb. hot Italian sausages, halved crosswise**
- 3 **Italian frying peppers or Cubanelles, halved lengthwise and seeded**
- 2 **large red bell peppers, cut into large strips**
- 2 **large red onions, cut into 1-inch wedges**
- 2 **Tbsp. extra-virgin olive oil, plus more for brushing**
- 2 **Tbsp. dried oregano**
  Kosher salt and pepper
  One 4-lb. whole chicken
- 2 **tsp. finely grated lemon zest**

1. Preheat the oven to 450°. Wrap the center pillar of a 10-inch Bundt pan with aluminum foil.

2. In a large bowl, toss the sausages with all of the peppers, the onions, the 2 tablespoons of olive oil and 1 table-spoon of the oregano. Season with salt and pepper and add to the pan.

3. Brush the chicken with olive oil and season with salt, pepper, the remaining 1 tablespoon of oregano and the lemon zest. Perch the chicken on the pan by inserting the center pillar into the cavity.

4. Roast the chicken for about 1 hour, until an instant-read thermometer inserted in an inner thigh registers 155°. Transfer to a cutting board and let rest for 15 minutes.

5. Transfer the sausages, peppers, onions and pan juices to a platter. Carve the chicken, arrange on the platter and serve right away.

SERVE WITH Crusty bread.

CONTINUED ▶

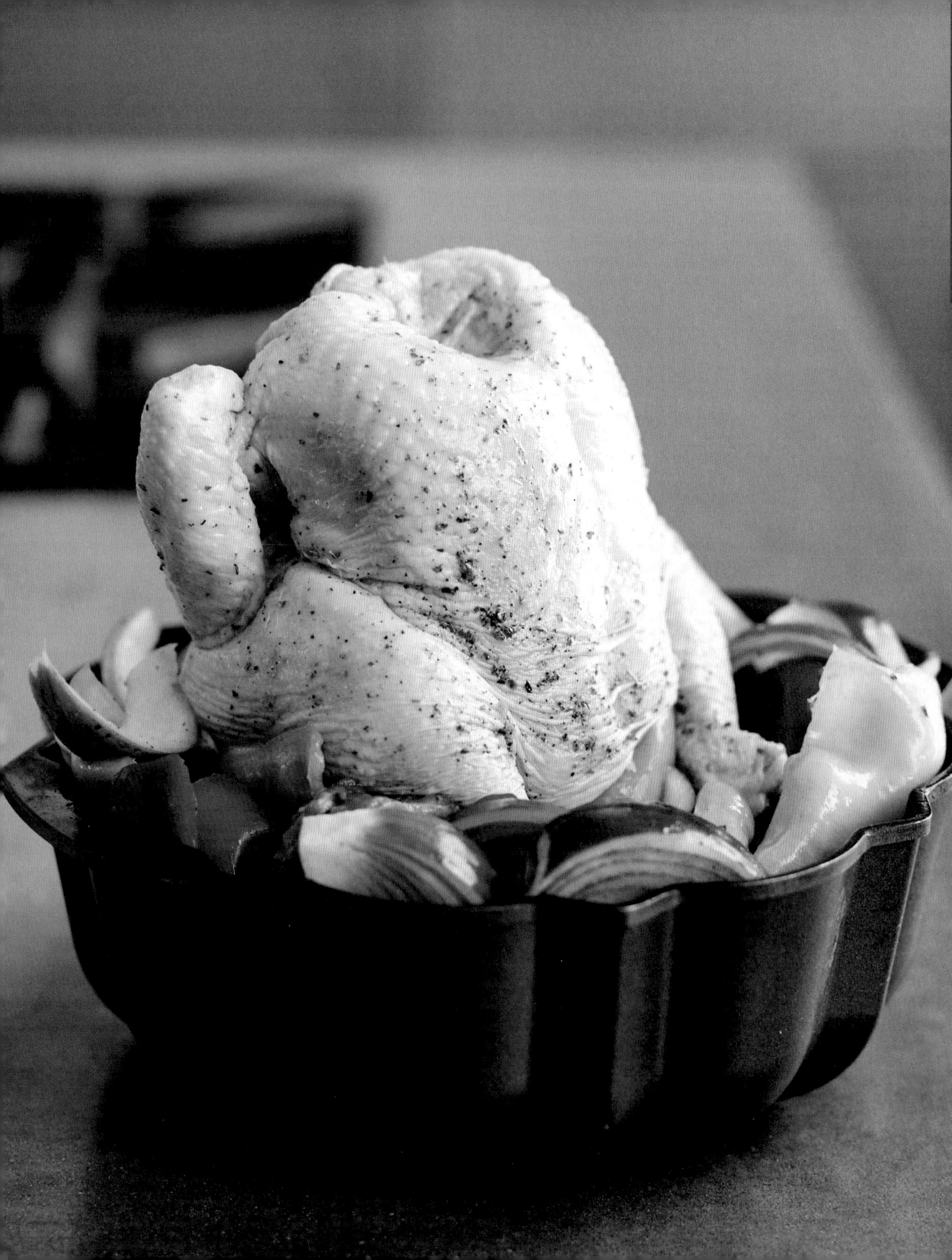

▶ CONTINUED

ROAST
CHICKEN

Buffalo-Style Roast Chicken with Potatoes

Active **30 min**; Total **1 hr 45 min**; Serves **4**

- 6 Tbsp. unsalted butter, melted
- ¼ cup hot sauce, such as Frank's RedHot
- Kosher salt and pepper
- 2 lbs. mixed baby red and Yukon Gold potatoes
- 6 large shallots, halved lengthwise
- 2 Tbsp. extra-virgin olive oil
- One 4-lb. whole chicken

1. Preheat the oven to 450°. In a small bowl, blend the butter, hot sauce and 1 teaspoon each of salt and pepper. Refrigerate until spreadable, about 10 minutes.

2. Wrap the center pillar of a 10-inch Bundt pan with foil. In a medium bowl, toss the potatoes and shallots with the olive oil and season generously with salt and pepper. Add to the pan.

3. Run your fingers under the breast and thigh skin of the chicken to loosen it, then spread the chilled butter under the skin and over the breast and thighs. Season with salt and pepper. Perch the chicken on the pan by inserting the center pillar into the cavity.

4. Roast the chicken in the center of the oven for about 1 hour, until browned and an instant-read thermometer inserted in an inner thigh registers 155°. Transfer to a cutting board and let rest for 15 minutes. Carve the chicken and serve with the potatoes and shallots.

MAKE AN ICE RING

Layer fruit in a Bundt pan. Add just enough distilled water to cover, then freeze. Dip the bottom of the pan in a large bowl of very hot water to loosen the ice ring. Invert it onto a plate and add it to any punch or sangria.

CONTINUED ▶

SANGRIA ICE RINGS
4 WAYS

The last thing I want to do when hosting a party is to get stuck fixing drinks all night. Instead, I make a big batch of sangria or punch. And since little ice cubes are going to melt quickly, I freeze an oversize ice ring filled with fruit in a Bundt pan. It keeps the punch chilled while also looking gorgeous in the bowl. Serve the sangria in glasses with or without ice cubes.

1 Vinho Verde Sangria with Mint and Cucumber Ice Ring

Thinly slice 3 **Persian cucumbers** lengthwise. Layer in a Bundt pan with 8 **mint sprigs** and 2 thinly sliced **limes.** Add just enough **distilled water** to cover. Freeze until solid, at least 8 hours or up to 3 days. In a large punch bowl, combine two 750-ml bottles **vinho verde,** two 12-oz. bottles **ginger beer,** 6 oz. **gin** and 1½ oz. **fresh lime juice.** Refrigerate the sangria until chilled, about 45 minutes. Fill a large bowl with very hot water. Dip the bottom of the Bundt pan in the water, then invert the ice ring onto a plate. Gently add the ice ring to the sangria. *Serves 6.*

3

4

3 Autumn Sangria with Apple and Pear Ice Ring

Cut 1 **Bartlett pear** into wedges and thinly slice 4 **Lady apples** lengthwise. Layer in a Bundt pan with 8 **cinnamon sticks** and 6 **star anise pods**. Add just enough **distilled water** to cover. Freeze until solid, at least 8 hours or up to 3 days. In a large punch bowl, combine two 750-ml bottles **Sancerre**, 16 oz. **all-natural apple juice**, 4 oz. **brandy**, 1 oz. **fresh lemon juice**, ½ tsp. **ground cinnamon** and a pinch each of **ground nutmeg** and **cloves**. Refrigerate the sangria until chilled, about 45 minutes. To serve, fill a large bowl with very hot water. Dip the bottom of the Bundt pan in the water, then invert the ice ring onto a plate. Gently add the ice ring to the sangria. *Serves 6.*

4 Winter Sangria with Citrus Ice Ring

In a Bundt pan, layer wedges of ½ **pink grapefruit** and ½ **Cara Cara** or other navel orange with thin slices of 2 **clementines**, 1 **blood orange** and 1 **lime**. Add just enough **distilled water** to cover the fruit. Freeze until solid, at least 8 hours or up to 3 days. In a large punch bowl, combine two 750-ml bottles **fruity red wine**, 8 oz. each of **fresh orange juice** and **fresh grapefruit juice**, 6 oz. **brandy**, 3 oz. **simple syrup** (see Rosé Sangria), 2 oz. **Cointreau** (or triple sec) and 1½ oz. **fresh lime juice**. Refrigerate the sangria until chilled, about 45 minutes. To serve, fill a large bowl with very hot water. Dip the bottom of the Bundt pan in the water, then invert the ice ring onto a plate. Gently add the ice ring to the sangria. *Serves 6.*

2 Rosé Sangria with Berry Ice Ring

In a Bundt pan, layer 1 cup sliced **strawberries** plus 3 cups other assorted **berries** and ½ cup **fresh currants**. Add just enough **distilled water** to cover the berries. Freeze until solid, at least 8 hours or up to 3 days. In a large punch bowl, combine two 750-ml bottles **rosé**, 8 oz. **white rum**, 8 oz. **simple syrup** (equal parts water and sugar boiled until dissolved, then cooled), 4 oz. **Campari** and 2 oz. **fresh lemon juice**. Refrigerate the sangria until chilled, 45 minutes. Fill a large bowl with very hot water. Dip the bottom of the pan in the water, then invert the ice ring onto a plate. Gently add the ring to the sangria. *Serves 6.*

BAKE A PASTA PIE

 Mix the pasta pie ingredients in a bowl, then bake in a Bundt pan—its grooves give you more crazy-crisp edges than a plain rectangular pan.

Pasta Bundt Loaf

Active **25 min;** Total **1 hr 20 min;** Serves **8**

This pasta pie is a fun riff on mac and cheese. I use three types of cheese here: Fontina and cheddar, which melt beautifully, as well as Parmigiano-Reggiano to create the crispest edges.

	Unsalted butter, for greasing
1	**lb. spaghetti**
6	**oz. Fontina cheese, shredded (2 cups)**
6	**oz. sharp white cheddar cheese, shredded (2 cups)**
1½	**cups whole milk**
¾	**cup freshly grated Parmigiano-Reggiano cheese**
3	**large eggs, lightly beaten**
2½	**tsp. pepper**
2	**tsp. kosher salt**

1. Preheat the oven to 425°. Generously butter a 10-inch Bundt pan. In a pot of salted boiling water, cook the spaghetti until al dente. Drain well.

2. In a large bowl, mix the pasta with the remaining ingredients. Scrape into the prepared pan. Bake until the cheese is melted and bubbling, 35 to 40 minutes.

3. Transfer the pasta Bundt loaf to a rack and let cool for 15 minutes. Invert the loaf onto a platter, cut into wedges and serve.

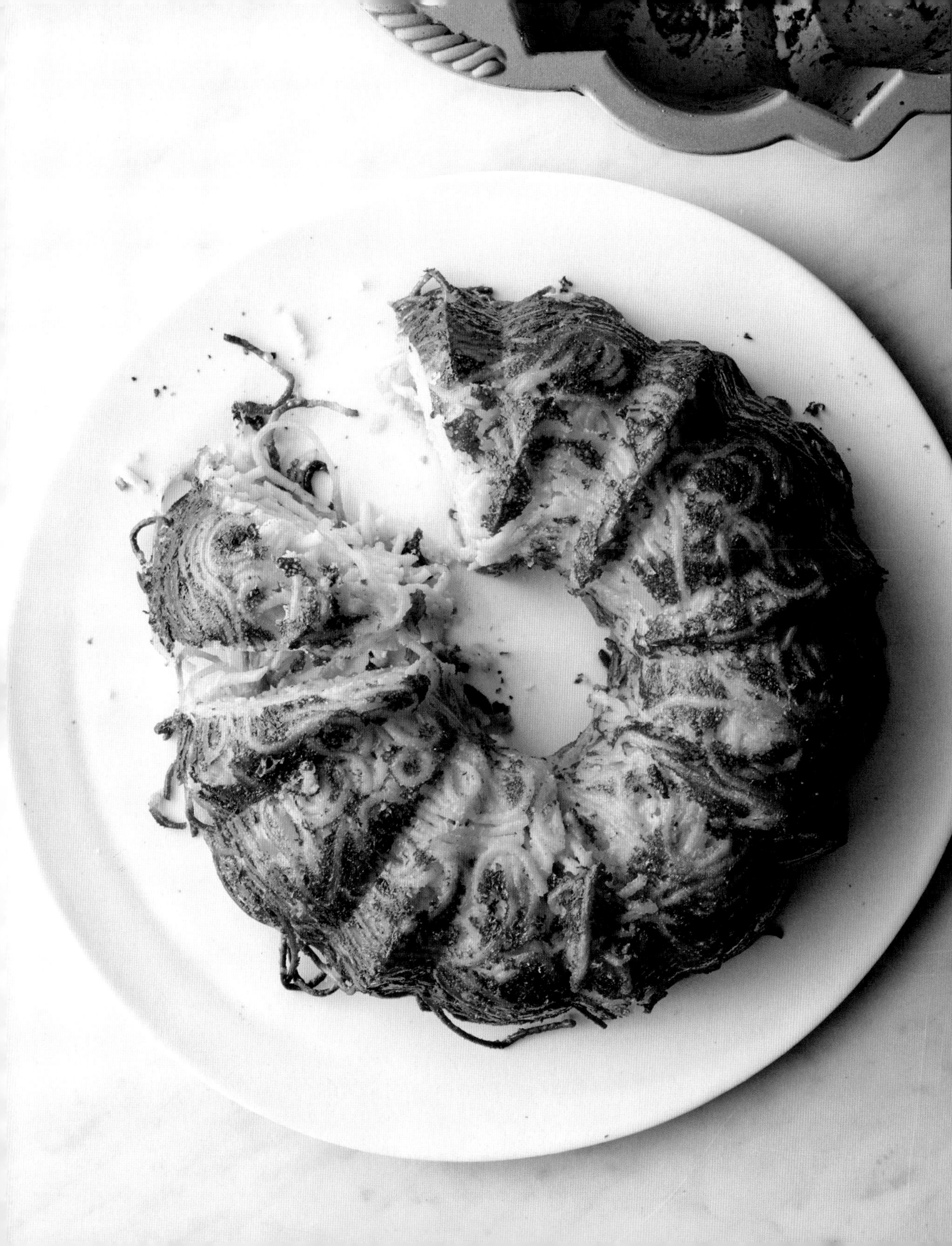

CHEESECLOTH

MAKE TEA BAGS

Of course you can easily buy tea bags, but I'm a DIY kind of guy. I love to customize my own tea bags so my tea tastes exactly how I want it to. Tied with pretty kitchen twine, these make great gifts. The recipe is for individual tea bags, but you could also pile the ingredients into one big bag for a pot of tea.

 Fill squares of cheesecloth with your tea blend. (A double layer will keep smaller ingredients from falling through.) Tie each tea bag closed with unflavored dental floss or thin kitchen twine.

Citrus and Green Tea Bags
Total **30 min**; Makes **8**

- **1 large organic lemon**
- **1 organic orange**
- **½ cup whole green tea leaves**

1. Using a vegetable peeler, peel off just the zest of the lemon and orange, avoiding the bitter white pith. Cut the zest into thin julienne. Spread half of the lemon and orange zests on a microwave-safe plate. Heat at high power in 30-second intervals until the zest is dry, 1 to 2 minutes. Repeat with the remaining zests.

2. On a work surface, spread out eight 3-by-3-inch double-layer squares of cheesecloth. Spoon 1 tablespoon of the green tea leaves and 2 teaspoons of the citrus zest on each square. Wrap the cheesecloth around the tea blend and tie closed with unflavored dental floss or thin kitchen twine.

3. To serve, cover the tea bag with boiling water and let steep for 3 to 5 minutes.

MAKE AHEAD The tea bags can be stored in an airtight container for up to 1 month.

3 more tea blends

Tie these blends in cheesecloth, then steep the tea bag in hot water for 3 to 5 minutes.

LEMON-MINT TEA I like to steep this caffeine-free combo double-strength, then serve it over ice in the summer. To make it, I dry mint sprigs and lemon peels in the microwave at high power in 20-second intervals.

CINNAMON-SPICE TEA I love this blend in the winter. The spices are warming and perfect for the holidays. The star anise and clove are accent flavors, so a tiny amount goes a long way. To make it, I combine broken cinnamon sticks, cracked star anise and a whole clove.

HIBISCUS GREEN TEA The hibiscus gives the tea a delicate floral flavor and the most gorgeous ruby-red color. The tea is delicious hot or iced. To make it, I mix dried hibiscus flowers with whole green tea leaves and dried lemon and lime peels.

BASTE TURKEY

Like you, my biggest fear when roasting a turkey is that it's going to be bland and dry. This tip is guaranteed to deliver a juicy, delicious bird every time. You drape the breast and legs with a cheesecloth that's soaked in melted flavored butter. Basically a turkey shawl! Once the bird is in the oven, I don't even have to touch it. All the butter and flavorings in the cloth will seep down into the turkey and baste it. After roasting, you'll see the turkey is golden with beautifully crisp skin.

 STEP 1 Dampen a double-layer length of cheesecloth with water and squeeze it dry.

STEP 2 Soak the cheesecloth in melted flavored butter.

STEP 3 Drape the cheesecloth over the turkey breast and legs.

STEP 4 Pour any remaining butter on top of the cheesecloth.

STEP 5 After roasting, carefully peel the cheesecloth off the turkey and discard.

CONTINUED ▶

▶ CONTINUED

BASTE
TURKEY

Citrus and Butter Turkey

Active **40 min**; Total **3 hr 30 min**; Serves **10**

> One 12- to 14-lb. turkey, rinsed and patted dry
>
> Kosher salt and pepper

1½ sticks unsalted butter

1½ Tbsp. finely grated grapefruit zest plus ¼ cup fresh grapefruit juice

1½ Tbsp. finely grated orange zest plus ¼ cup fresh orange juice

1½ Tbsp. finely grated lemon zest plus 3 Tbsp. fresh lemon juice

4 garlic cloves, finely grated

1 Tbsp. minced thyme plus 5 sprigs

½ grapefruit, cut into wedges

½ orange, cut into wedges

1 lemon, cut into wedges

3 cups chicken stock

1. Season the turkey inside and out with salt and pepper. Transfer to a rack set in a roasting pan; bring to room temperature.

2. Preheat the oven to 400°. In a medium saucepan, melt the butter. Whisk in the citrus zests and juices, garlic and minced thyme; let cool slightly. Transfer half of the citrus butter to a small bowl and refrigerate until spreadable, 20 minutes.

3. Run your fingers under the breast and thigh skin to loosen it, then spread the chilled butter under the skin and over the breast and thighs. Stuff the turkey cavity with the thyme sprigs and citrus wedges. Dampen an 18-by-18-inch double layer of cheesecloth with water and squeeze dry. Soak the cheesecloth in the remaining citrus butter and drape it over the breast and legs; pour any remaining butter on top.

4. Roast the turkey for about 30 minutes. Add the stock to the roasting pan and continue to roast for about 1 hour and 45 minutes longer, rotating the pan a few times, until an instant-read thermometer inserted in an inner thigh registers 165°.

5. Carefully peel the cheesecloth off the turkey. Transfer the turkey to a cutting board and let rest for 30 minutes. Skim the fat off the pan juices and transfer to a gravy bowl. Carve the turkey and serve with the pan juices.

Chipotle-Butter Turkey

Active **40 min**; Total **3 hr 30 min**; Serves **10**

> One 12- to 14-lb. turkey, rinsed and patted dry
>
> Kosher salt and pepper

2 sticks unsalted butter

½ cup distilled white vinegar

⅓ cup minced chipotle chiles in adobo

2 Tbsp. minced garlic

1 Tbsp. dried oregano

1 Tbsp. chopped thyme plus 4 sprigs

1 head of garlic, halved crosswise

1 lime, quartered

4 oregano sprigs

3 cups chicken stock

1. Season the turkey inside and out with salt and pepper. Transfer to a rack set in a roasting pan; bring to room temperature.

2. Meanwhile, preheat the oven to 400°. In a medium saucepan, melt the butter. Whisk in the vinegar, chipotles, minced garlic, dried oregano and chopped thyme; let cool slightly. Transfer half of the chipotle butter to a small bowl and refrigerate until spreadable, about 20 minutes.

3. Run your fingers under the turkey breast and thigh skin to loosen it, then spread the chilled butter under the skin and over the breast and thighs. Stuff the turkey cavity with the head of garlic, the lime wedges and the thyme and oregano sprigs. Dampen an 18-by-18-inch double-layer piece of cheesecloth with water and squeeze dry. Soak the cheesecloth in the remaining chipotle butter and drape it over the breast and legs; pour any remaining butter on top.

4. Roast the turkey for about 30 minutes. Add the stock to the roasting pan and continue to roast for about 1 hour and 45 minutes longer, rotating the pan a few times, until an instant-read thermometer inserted in an inner thigh registers 165°.

5. Carefully peel the cheesecloth off the turkey. Transfer the turkey to a cutting board and let rest for 30 minutes. Skim the fat off the pan juices and transfer to a gravy bowl. Carve the turkey and serve with the pan juices.

Soy and Sesame Turkey

Active **40 min**; Total **3 hr 30 min**; Serves **10**

> One 12- to 14-lb. turkey, rinsed and patted dry
>
> Kosher salt and black pepper

1½ sticks unsalted butter

½ cup plus 2 Tbsp. soy sauce

½ cup plus 2 Tbsp. toasted sesame oil

½ cup minced scallions plus 6 whole scallions

¼ cup light brown sugar

3 Tbsp. finely grated peeled fresh ginger, plus one 3-inch piece, thinly sliced

1 tsp. crushed red pepper

3 cups chicken stock

1. Season the turkey inside and out with salt and black pepper. Transfer the turkey to a rack set in a roasting pan and let come to room temperature.

2. Preheat the oven to 400°. In a medium saucepan, melt the butter. Whisk in the soy sauce, sesame oil, minced scallions, sugar, grated ginger and crushed red pepper; let cool slightly. Transfer half of the flavored butter to a small bowl; refrigerate until spreadable, about 20 minutes.

3. Run your fingers under the turkey breast and thigh skin to loosen it, then spread the chilled butter under the skin and over the breast and thighs. Stuff the turkey cavity with the whole scallions and sliced ginger. Dampen an 18-by-18-inch double layer piece of cheesecloth with water and squeeze dry. Soak the cheesecloth in the remaining flavored butter and drape it over the breast and legs; pour any remaining butter on top.

4. Roast the turkey for about 30 minutes. Add the stock to the roasting pan and continue to roast for about 1 hour and 45 minutes longer, rotating the pan a few times, until an instant-read thermometer inserted in an inner thigh registers 165°.

5. Carefully peel the cheesecloth off the turkey. Transfer the turkey to a cutting board and let rest for 30 minutes. Skim the fat off the pan juices and transfer to a gravy bowl. Carve the turkey and serve with the pan juices.

DIY A POWDERED SUGAR SHAKER

 Line a small bowl with a 5-by-5-inch single-layer piece of cheesecloth. Add ¼ cup of confectioners' sugar. Tie the cloth closed with unflavored dental floss or kitchen twine. Use to dust cookies, cakes or hot chocolate.

Lime-Scented Linzer Cookies

Active **1 hr;** Total **2 hr 45 min plus cooling;** Makes **2 dozen**

- 2 **cups all-purpose flour, plus more for dusting**
- ½ **cup almond meal**
-    **Kosher salt**
- 2 **sticks unsalted butter, softened**
- ⅔ **cup granulated sugar**
- 1 **tsp. pure vanilla extract**
- 2 **tsp. packed finely grated lime zest**
-    **Confectioners' sugar, for dusting**
- ½ **cup raspberry jam**
- 2 **tsp. fresh lime juice**

1. In a medium bowl, whisk the 2 cups of flour with the almond meal and ¾ teaspoon of salt. In a stand mixer fitted with the paddle or in a large bowl using a hand mixer, beat the butter with the granulated sugar at medium speed until creamy. Add the vanilla and 1 teaspoon of the lime zest and beat until smooth. Add the dry ingredients and beat at low speed until smooth. Pat the dough into 2 disks, wrap in plastic and refrigerate until well chilled, about 1 hour.

2. Preheat the oven to 350° and line 2 large baking sheets with parchment paper. Working in batches if necessary, roll out the dough ¼ inch thick on a lightly floured surface. Using a 2-inch round cutter, stamp out cookies as close together as possible. Using a smaller decorative cookie cutter, stamp out the centers of half of the cookies. Transfer the whole cookies to 1 prepared baking sheet and the cutout cookies to the other. Reroll the scraps and stamp out more cookies. Refrigerate the cookies until well chilled, about 30 minutes.

3. Bake the cookies in the upper and middle thirds of the oven for 17 to 20 minutes, until very lightly browned around the edges and just firm; shift the pans from top to bottom and front to back halfway through baking. Let cool on the baking sheets.

4. Dust the tops of the cutout cookies generously with confectioners' sugar. In a small bowl, whisk the raspberry jam with the remaining 1 teaspoon of lime zest, the lime juice and a pinch of salt. Spoon 1 teaspoon of the jam mixture onto each whole cookie, cover with the sugar-dusted cookies and serve.

MAKE AHEAD The cookies can be stored in an airtight container for up to 5 days.

JUICE CITRUS

Not only does this retro cheesecloth hack get you loads of juice without a reamer, it's fantastic for juicing citrus that's too large for a standard reamer, like oranges and grapefruit. And the best part? The seeds stay in the cheesecloth, so you don't have to strain or pick them out.

Wrap citrus halves with a damp double layer of cheesecloth. Squeeze to release juice without any pulp or seeds.

Boozy Tangerine Pops

Total **30 min plus 5 hr freezing**
Makes **6**

⅓ **cup sugar**

   6 to 8 tangerines, halved crosswise

3 **Tbsp. gin**

2 **Tbsp. fresh lime juice**

1. In a small saucepan, combine the sugar and ⅓ cup of water and bring to a boil, stirring to dissolve the sugar. Let the simple syrup cool completely.

2. Wrap a tangerine half with a damp double layer of cheesecloth and squeeze over a medium bowl to release all of the juice. Repeat with the remaining tangerine halves. You should have 1½ cups of juice. Discard the cheesecloth with the seeds and pulp.

3. Whisk the gin, lime juice and cooled simple syrup into the tangerine juice. Pour the mixture into six 6-ounce popsicle molds and freeze until firm but not solid, about 1 hour. Insert popsicle sticks and freeze until firm, at least 4 hours and preferably overnight.

MAKE AHEAD The pops can be frozen for up to 1 week.

Roasted Lemon and Bay Leaf Hard Lemonade

Total **35 min plus 1 hr chilling; Serves 6**

3 **lemons, quartered lengthwise, plus 6 wheels for garnish**

9 **fresh bay leaves**

1¼ **cups simple syrup (see Note)**

1 **cup plus 2 Tbsp. vodka**

   Ice

1 **cup plus 2 Tbsp. club soda**

1. Preheat the oven to 400°. In a small roasting pan, roast the lemon quarters with 3 of the bay leaves for about 20 minutes, until the lemons are softened and browned in spots.

2. Line a medium bowl with a large double layer of damp cheesecloth. Scrape the lemons, bay leaves and any pan juices into the lined bowl and let cool slightly. Wrap the cheesecloth around the lemon mixture and squeeze firmly to release as much juice as possible; twist the cheesecloth occasionally while squeezing. Discard the cheesecloth and solids.

3. Transfer the juice to a large pitcher. Add 2 cups of water, the simple syrup and the vodka; stir well. Refrigerate until chilled, about 1 hour. Pour the drink into 6 ice-filled collins glasses. Top each drink with 3 tablespoons of club soda and garnish with a lemon wheel and bay leaf.

NOTE To make simple syrup, combine 1 cup sugar and 1 cup water in a small saucepan and bring to a boil, stirring to dissolve the sugar. Let cool completely before using. Makes about 1½ cups.

COOKIE CUTTERS

STAMP OUT CROUTONS

I try to take every opportunity to make meals more fun. That's where cookie cutters come in handy! Instead of cutting bread into plain old squares for croutons, I use decorative cutters to stamp out different shapes: clovers for St. Patrick's Day, hearts for Valentine's Day and stars for just about every other occasion. Kids especially love these designer croutons.

 Stamp out bread shapes with decorative cookie cutters. Sprinkle with cheese and bake.

Tomato Soup with Cheesy Croutons

Active **30 min**; Total **1 hr 30 min**; Serves **4**

- **3 lbs. plum tomatoes, cored and halved lengthwise**
- **6 unpeeled shallots, halved lengthwise**
- **6 unpeeled garlic cloves, crushed**
- **2 basil sprigs, plus leaves for garnish**
- **3 thyme sprigs**
- **¼ cup extra-virgin olive oil**
- **Kosher salt and black pepper**
- **One 14-oz. can diced tomatoes**
- **4 Tbsp. unsalted butter, cubed**
- **1 cup chicken stock or low-sodium broth**
- **Pinch each of cayenne pepper and sugar**
- **Four ½-inch-thick slices of sourdough boule**
- **Shredded Gruyère cheese, for sprinkling**

1. Preheat the oven to 400°. On a large rimmed baking sheet, toss the plum tomatoes with the shallots, garlic, basil and thyme sprigs and olive oil. Season generously with salt and black pepper and toss again. Bake for about 45 minutes, stirring halfway through, until the tomatoes are tender. Leave the oven on.

2. Discard the tomato, shallot and garlic skins as well as the herb sprigs. Scrape the tomato mixture into a blender. Add the canned tomatoes and butter and puree until very smooth. Transfer the pureed tomatoes to a large saucepan, then whisk in the chicken stock, cayenne and sugar. Cook over moderate heat, stirring occasionally, until hot, about 8 minutes. Season with salt and black pepper. Keep warm over very low heat.

3. Meanwhile, using decorative cookie cutters, stamp out sourdough shapes. Reserve the crusts and any scraps for bread crumbs. Transfer the bread to a baking sheet and sprinkle each shape with a little shredded Gruyère. Bake for about 12 minutes, until golden and crisp.

4. Ladle the tomato soup into bowls, top with the cheesy croutons and basil leaves and serve.

MAKE AHEAD The soup can be refrigerated for up to 3 days. Reheat gently.

VARIATION For a toad-in-the-hole, stamp out the center of a slice of bread. Melt butter in a skillet. Add the bread slice and the stamped-out shape. Crack an egg into the hole in the bread and cook for about 2 minutes. Carefully flip the bread and the stamped-out shape, add more butter and cook for another 2 minutes. Transfer to a plate and serve.

DECORATE CAKES

If you don't have a pastry bag (or aren't a pro with one), this is my foolproof way to decorate cakes. I like to play with different shapes and colors to create a striking dessert. Tag me with yours on Instagram!

 Gently press cookie cutters onto a freshly frosted cake. Fill each cutter with sprinkles. Remove the cutters to reveal a gorgeous decoration.

Rainy Day Carrot Cake

Active **50 min;** Total **3 hr;** Serves **12**

CAKE

- 2 **sticks unsalted butter, softened, plus more for greasing**
- 1 **cup walnuts**
- 2 **cups all-purpose flour**
- 2 **tsp. cinnamon**
- 2 **tsp. baking powder**
- 1½ **tsp. kosher salt**
- 1 **tsp. baking soda**
- 1 **tsp. ground ginger**
- ¼ **tsp. freshly grated nutmeg**
- 2 **cups granulated sugar**
- 4 **large eggs**
- 1 **cup buttermilk**
- ¼ **cup canola oil**
- 1 **Tbsp. pure vanilla extract**
- 2½ **cups shredded carrots (about 8 oz.)**

FROSTING

- 1½ **lbs. cream cheese, at room temperature**
- 1½ **sticks unsalted butter, at room temperature**
- 2¼ **cups confectioners' sugar**
- ¾ **tsp. pure vanilla extract**
  Finely ground toasted walnuts or sprinkles, for decorating

1. Make the cake Preheat the oven to 350°. Butter a 9-by-13-inch metal baking pan. Line the pan with foil. Spread the walnuts in a pie plate and toast for 8 to 10 minutes, until golden and fragrant. Let cool, then coarsely chop.

2. In a medium bowl, whisk the flour with the cinnamon, baking powder, salt, baking soda, ginger and nutmeg. In a stand mixer fitted with the paddle or in a large bowl using a hand mixer, beat the 2 sticks of butter with the granulated sugar at medium speed until fluffy, about 2 minutes. Beat in the eggs one at a time, then beat in the buttermilk, oil and vanilla until incorporated. Beat in the dry ingredients at low speed until just incorporated, then stir in the carrots and toasted walnuts. Scrape the batter into the prepared pan and bake for about 45 minutes, until a toothpick inserted in the center of the cake comes out clean. Let cool completely in the pan.

3. Meanwhile, make the frosting In a stand mixer fitted with the paddle or in a large bowl using a hand mixer, beat the cream cheese with the butter until smooth. Beat in the confectioners' sugar and vanilla at low speed until nearly incorporated, then beat at medium speed until smooth.

4. Invert the cake onto a large baking sheet, peel off the foil, then invert the cake onto a platter. Spread the frosting evenly on the top and sides of the cake. Gently press decorative cookie cutters on top. Fill each cutter with a thin layer of ground toasted walnuts or sprinkles. Carefully remove the cookie cutters, cut the cake into squares and serve.

MAKE AHEAD The cake can be refrigerated in an airtight container for 5 days.

SHAPE WHIPPED CREAM

I love a dollop of fresh whipped cream in my hot cocoa, but the problem is that it melts right away. With my tip for frozen whipped cream shapes, you get an unexpected garnish that stays intact while you sip.

 Freeze whipped cream on a foil-lined rimmed baking sheet. Stamp out shapes with decorative cookie cutters.

Rich and Creamy Hot Chocolate with Frozen Whipped Cream

Active **15 min**; Total **1 hr 15 min**; Serves **4**

1¾ cups heavy cream

2 Tbsp. confectioners' sugar

¼ tsp. pure vanilla extract

2½ cups whole milk

½ cup granulated sugar

Pinch of kosher salt

7 oz. bittersweet chocolate, finely chopped

1. In a large bowl, using a hand mixer, beat 1 cup of the heavy cream with the confectioners' sugar and vanilla until thick. Spread the whipped cream in a ½-inch-thick layer on a foil-lined rimmed baking sheet. Freeze until firm, about 1 hour. Slide the foil onto a work surface. Using decorative cookie cutters, stamp out shapes and return them to the baking sheet. Keep frozen until serving.

2. Meanwhile, in a medium saucepan, combine the remaining ¾ cup of heavy cream with the milk, granulated sugar and salt. Bring just to a simmer. Remove from the heat and add the chocolate. Let stand for 2 minutes, then stir until smooth. Keep warm over low heat, stirring occasionally. To serve, ladle the hot chocolate into mugs and top with a frozen whipped cream shape.

MAKE AHEAD The frozen whipped cream can be frozen in an airtight container for up to 1 week.

3 more whipped cream ideas for hot cocoa

MINI SHAPES Use small cookie cutters to stamp out adorable miniature whipped cream shapes.

COLORED SHAPES Add strawberry preserves to whipped cream and use a skewer to create a cool swirled pattern before freezing. Alternatively, mix a drop or two of red or blue food coloring into whipped cream before freezing. These shapes look especially good in white hot chocolate because they'll slowly tint the drink as they melt.

SPICED Get creative with spices. Try mixing ground cardamom or cinnamon into whipped cream before freezing. Or instant espresso for a mocha-style hot chocolate.

MAKE WHITE CHOCOLATE CANDIES

Spread melted white chocolate on an aluminum foil–lined baking sheet. After it firms up, stamp out bite-size candies with cookie cutters.

DIY White Chocolate Candies

Active **20 min;** Total **1 hr 5 min**
Makes **about 44**

Forget the double boiler: One of the easiest ways to melt chocolate is in the microwave. After stamping out your candy shapes, you can remelt the white chocolate scraps to make even more.

1 **lb. white chocolate, finely chopped**

Purple food coloring, matcha powder, cocoa powder, rose petals or lavender flowers, for decorating (see directions opposite)

In a large microwave-safe bowl, heat the white chocolate at high power in 20-second intervals until nearly melted. Let stand for 2 minutes, then stir until smooth. Using a small offset spatula, spread the white chocolate in a scant ¼-inch-thick layer on a foil-lined baking sheet. Let stand until firm, about 45 minutes. Using 1-inch-wide cutters, stamp out candies and transfer them to a plate.

VARIATION See the three ideas on the opposite page.

turn plain chocolate into eye candy

MARBLING To make swirled white chocolate candies, mix ¼ cup of the melted white chocolate with 2 drops of purple food coloring until no streaks remain. Using a small offset spatula, spread the remaining melted white chocolate in a scant ¼-inch-thick layer on a foil-lined baking sheet. Drop spoonfuls of the purple chocolate on top of the white chocolate and, using a skewer, make decorative swirls. Let stand until firm, about 45 minutes. Using 1-inch-wide cutters, stamp out candies and transfer them to a plate.

EDIBLE FLOWERS Using a small offset spatula, spread the white chocolate in a scant ¼-inch-thick layer on a foil-lined baking sheet. Sprinkle with dried rose petals or lavender flowers. Let stand until firm, about 45 minutes. Using 1-inch-wide cutters, stamp out candies and transfer them to a plate.

MATCHA OR COCOA POWDER Using a small offset spatula, spread the white chocolate in a scant ¼-inch-thick layer on a foil-lined baking sheet. Let stand until firm, about 45 minutes. Using 1-inch-wide cutters, stamp out candies and transfer them to a baking sheet. Dust with matcha or cocoa and serve.

FLOSS

TRUSS CHICKEN

Trussing a chicken keeps the drumsticks and wings close to the body, which ensures even cooking. But if you don't have kitchen twine, you can just use plain dental floss. Yes, you can cook with it–just make sure it's unflavored!

 STEP 1 Place the chicken on a cutting board, breast side up. Tuck the wing tips under the body and face the legs away from you.

STEP 2 Take a piece of floss three times the length of the chicken and center it under the tail. Tie the legs together in a double knot.

STEP 3 Pull both ends of the floss around the sides of the bird toward you so that each piece runs between the drumstick and the thigh.

STEP 4 Flip the bird over and pull the floss tight around each wing. Tie a double knot at the neck. Trim the excess floss.

Green Curry Roast Chicken

Active **15 min**; Total **1 hr 15 min**; Serves **4**

- **4 Tbsp. unsalted butter, softened**
- **4 Tbsp. Thai green curry paste**
- **1½ tsp. finely grated lime zest**
- **Kosher salt and pepper**
- **One 3½-lb. whole chicken, trussed**
- **Lime wedges, for serving**

1. Preheat the oven to 425°. In a small bowl, using a fork, blend the butter with the curry paste, lime zest and a generous pinch each of salt and pepper. Carefully loosen the skin on the chicken breast and legs with your fingers. Spread the paste under the skin, gently pressing to even it out. Season the chicken all over with salt and pepper and transfer breast side up to a large ovenproof skillet.

2. Roast the chicken for about 50 minutes, until an instant-read thermometer inserted in an inner thigh registers 165°. Let rest for 10 minutes, then carve the chicken and serve with lime wedges.

SERVE WITH Steamed rice.

3 more butters for your bird

MIDDLE EASTERN One of my favorite street foods in New York City is shwarma (thin slices of spit-roasted meat, usually in a pita). Those seasonings inspired a spiced butter for roast chicken. To make it, I use a fork to blend softened butter with ground cumin, hot paprika, turmeric, allspice, garlic powder, cinnamon, black pepper and salt.

PROVENÇAL I like to borrow flavors from Provence for a wonderful chicken that evokes the south of France. To make it, I use a fork to blend softened butter with olive tapenade, minced fresh rosemary and finely grated lemon zest and garlic.

CITRUS Chicken and citrus love each other. A combo of different citrus zests with butter and garlic is delicious any time of year. To make it, I use a fork to blend softened butter with finely grated garlic and zest of orange, grapefruit, lemon and lime, then I season with salt and black pepper.

SLICE SOFT CHEESE

The thing about soft cheese is that it's messy to cut. Using a knife can mash it and make it stick to the blade. But with floss, you get clean, even slices every time. This is an awesome trick for cutting rounds from a log of fresh goat cheese. It also works like a charm on Brie, Camembert and fresh mozzarella.

 Place a long string of unflavored dental floss under the cheese. Cross the floss, then pull each end through the cheese to slice it.

Beet and Crispy Goat Cheese Sandwiches

Total **45 min;** Serves **4**

> One 9-oz. log of fresh goat cheese
>
> 2 **large eggs**
>
> Kosher salt and pepper
>
> 1½ **cups panko**
>
> 3 **medium steamed beets (not canned), thinly sliced**
>
> 1 **Tbsp. fresh lemon juice**
>
> 1 **Tbsp. extra-virgin olive oil, plus more for frying**
>
> 2 **Tbsp. minced chives**
>
> 8 **slices of seeded Jewish rye bread, lightly toasted or grilled (see Note)**
>
> 1 **cup baby spinach leaves**

1. Using unflavored dental floss, slice the cheese into ⅓-inch-thick rounds and transfer them to a plate. In a shallow bowl, beat the eggs with a pinch each of salt and pepper. Spread the panko in another shallow bowl and season with salt and pepper. Dip the cheese rounds in the egg, then dredge in the panko, pressing to help it adhere. Transfer the coated cheese rounds to a plate and freeze until firm, about 15 minutes.

2. Meanwhile, in a medium bowl, toss the beet slices with the lemon juice, 1 table-spoon of olive oil and the chives. Season the beets with salt and pepper.

3. In a large skillet, heat ¼ inch of olive oil until shimmering. Add half of the goat cheese rounds and cook over moderately high heat, turning once, until golden and crisp, about 3 minutes. Transfer to paper towels and repeat with the remaining cheese rounds.

4. Top 4 slices of the toast with the baby spinach, marinated beets and their juices and the crispy goat cheese. Close the sandwiches and serve them right away.

NOTE To grill the bread, heat a grill pan. Brush the bread with olive oil and grill over moderately high heat, turning once, until lightly charred, about 2 minutes.

MAKE AHEAD The marinated beets can be refrigerated overnight.

LIFT FRAGILE COOKIES

Slide unflavored dental floss under cookies or little cakes like these to loosen them from a baking sheet without breaking.

Gingerbread Whoopie Pies

Active **40 min**; Total **1 hr 30 min**; Makes **16**

CAKES

2½ **cups all-purpose flour**

  1 **Tbsp. plus 2 tsp. ground ginger**

1½ **tsp. cinnamon**

  1 **tsp. baking soda**

½ **tsp. baking powder**

½ **tsp. kosher salt**

¼ **tsp. freshly grated nutmeg**

¼ **tsp. ground cloves**

  1 **stick unsalted butter, softened**

  1 **cup packed dark brown sugar**

  1 **large egg**

  6 **Tbsp. unsulfured molasses**

  1 **tsp. pure vanilla extract**

¾ **cup buttermilk**

FILLING

2½ **sticks unsalted butter, softened**

2½ **cups confectioners' sugar**

  2 **tsp. finely grated lemon zest
     plus 1 Tbsp. fresh lemon juice**

1. Make the cakes Preheat the oven
to 350°. Line 2 large baking sheets with
parchment paper. In a medium bowl,
whisk the flour, ginger, cinnamon, baking
soda, baking powder, salt, nutmeg and
cloves. In a large bowl, using a hand
mixer, beat the butter and brown sugar
at medium speed until fluffy, 2 minutes.
Beat in the egg, molasses and vanilla.
At low speed, beat in the dry ingredients
and buttermilk in 3 alternating additions;
scrape down the bowl as necessary.

2. Using a 2-tablespoon ice cream scoop,
scoop 16 level mounds of dough onto each
sheet, 1½ inches apart. Bake in the lower
and upper thirds of the oven for 12 to 14
minutes, until risen and firm; shift the
pans halfway through. Transfer the sheets
to racks; let the cakes cool completely.

3. Make the filling In a large bowl, beat
the butter with the confectioners' sugar
and lemon zest and juice until smooth.
Spoon the filling onto the flat sides of 16
of the cakes and close the whoopie pies,
pressing to distribute the filling to the
edges. Transfer to a platter and refrigerate until barely chilled, 15 minutes.

1

CUT LAYER CAKES

Use floss to make the most precise cuts for beautiful layer cakes.

 STEP 1 With a ruler, measure the center of the cake. Insert six toothpicks in the midpoint evenly around the cake.

STEPS 2 AND 3 Wrap floss around the cake using the toothpicks as a guide. Cross the floss and pull the ends through the cake.

2

3

Chocolate Layer Cake with Strawberry Buttercream

Active **1 hr 15 min**; Total **3 hr plus cooling**
Serves **12**

CAKE

- 6 **Tbsp. unsalted butter, cubed, plus more for greasing**
- 1¾ **cups all-purpose flour, plus more for dusting**
- 1¾ **cups granulated sugar**
- ¼ **cup unsweetened cocoa powder**
- 2 **tsp. baking powder**
- 1¾ **tsp. baking soda**
- 1 **tsp. kosher salt**
- 1¾ **cups whole milk**
- 3½ **oz. semisweet chocolate, finely chopped**
- 2 **large eggs**
- 2 **tsp. pure vanilla extract**

FROSTING

- 1 **lb. unsalted butter, at room temperature**
- 5 **cups confectioners' sugar (1¼ lbs.)**

  One 12-oz. jar strawberry preserves, at room temperature

  Pinch of kosher salt

1. Make the cake Preheat the oven to 350°. Butter two 8-inch round cake pans and line them with parchment paper. Dust the inside rims of the pans with flour, tapping out any excess.

2. In a large bowl, whisk the 1¾ cups of flour with the granulated sugar, cocoa powder, baking powder, baking soda and salt. In a medium saucepan, bring the milk just to a simmer. Remove from the heat and add the chocolate and 6 tablespoons of butter. Let stand for 2 minutes, then whisk until smooth. Whisk the warm milk mixture into the dry ingredients until just incorporated, then beat in the eggs and vanilla until fully incorporated.

3. Scrape the batter into the prepared pans. Bake for about 45 minutes, until a toothpick inserted in the center of each cake comes out clean. Let the cakes cool in the pans, then invert them onto a work surface. Peel off the parchment.

4. Using unflavored dental floss, slice each cake into 2 layers. Transfer the layers to baking sheets.

5. Make the frosting In a stand mixer fitted with the whisk, beat the butter with the confectioners' sugar at low speed until just incorporated, then beat at medium speed until smooth.

Add the strawberry preserves and salt and beat until fluffy and smooth; scrape down the side of the bowl as needed.

6. Set 1 cake layer on a plate. Spread the top with ¾ cup of the frosting. Top with the second layer and another ¾ cup of the frosting. Repeat the layering one more time and then set the final cake layer on top. Spread 1 cup of the frosting over the top and side of the cake in a thin layer. Refrigerate until the frosting is firm, about 30 minutes. Spread the remaining frosting all over the top and side of the cake. Refrigerate for 30 minutes before slicing.

FOOD PROCESSOR

BLEND HOLLANDAISE SAUCE

A classic hollandaise is one of the hardest sauces to master. Typically, you heat egg yolks over a double boiler, then very slowly whisk in clarified butter until the sauce is emulsified. With my hack, you'll get a velvety, rich hollandaise without stressing about curdled eggs or all that whisking.

To make an easy hollandaise sauce, slowly add melted butter to egg yolks and lemon juice in a food processor or blender.

Eggs Florentine with Smoky Hollandaise Sauce

Total **40 min**; Serves **6**

- **1** dozen large eggs
  Kosher salt and pepper
- **3** Tbsp. extra-virgin olive oil
- **1** large shallot, minced
- **2** garlic cloves, minced
- **20** oz. baby spinach
- **2½** sticks unsalted butter
- **4** large egg yolks
- **3½** Tbsp. fresh lemon juice
- **1** tsp. sweet pimentón de la Vera (smoked Spanish paprika)
- **6** English muffins, split and toasted
  Snipped chives, for garnish

1. Preheat the oven to 350°. Pour 1 tablespoon of water into each cup of a 12-cup muffin tin. Crack the eggs into the cups and bake for 13 to 15 minutes, until the whites are firm but the yolks are still runny. Using a slotted spoon, transfer the poached eggs to a paper towel–lined plate and season lightly with salt and pepper.

2. Meanwhile, in a large saucepan, heat the olive oil. Add the shallot and garlic and cook over moderately high until softened, about 2 minutes. Add the spinach in batches and cook, stirring, until just wilted, 3 to 5 minutes. Season the spinach with salt and pepper.

3. In a small saucepan, melt the butter. In a food processor or blender, combine the egg yolks, lemon juice and pimentón with 2 tablespoons of water and puree until smooth. With the machine on, gradually drizzle in the hot butter until the sauce is thick, about 1 minute. Season the hollandaise with salt and pepper.

4. Arrange the English muffins on plates or a platter. Mound the spinach on the English muffins and top with the poached eggs. Spoon the smoky hollandaise sauce over the eggs and garnish with chives. Serve right away.

CHURN
SOFT SERVE

You can make near-instant soft serve without an ice cream maker.

 STEP 1 Add frozen fruit to the bowl of a food processor.

STEP 2 Puree the fruit with condensed milk until smooth.

STEP 3 Serve soft or transfer to a metal baking pan and freeze until just firm.

1

2

3

Almost-Instant Soft Serve

Total **15 min**; Makes 3½ cups

1½ lbs. frozen strawberries, mangoes or blueberries

¾ cup sweetened condensed milk

½ tsp. pure vanilla extract

Kosher salt

In a food processor, pulse the fruit with the condensed milk, vanilla and a generous pinch of salt until the fruit is finely chopped. Puree until smooth, 2 to 3 minutes; scrape down the side of the bowl as needed. Serve soft or, for more of a sherbet-like texture, transfer to a metal baking pan, cover and freeze until just firm.

MAKE AHEAD The soft serve can be frozen for up to 3 days. Let stand at room temperature for 10 minutes before serving.

PREPARE CAULIFLOWER RICE

STEP 1 Core and cut cauliflower into florets.

STEP 2 Transfer to a food processor.

STEP 3 Pulse the cauliflower until the pieces are finely chopped and resemble rice.

Stir-Fried Cauliflower "Rice"

Total **35 min;** Serves **4**

1¾ lbs. cauliflower, cored and cut into 1½-inch florets

⅓ cup canola oil

3 Tbsp. minced peeled fresh ginger

3 Tbsp. minced garlic

1 cup chopped cilantro, plus more for garnish

2 fresh hot red chiles, thinly sliced

3 Tbsp. soy sauce

2 Tbsp. fresh lime juice

Kosher salt

In a food processor, pulse the cauliflower until finely chopped. In a large skillet, heat the oil until shimmering. Add the ginger and garlic and stir-fry over high heat until fragrant, about 1 minute. Add the cauliflower and stir-fry until crisp-tender, about 4 minutes. Stir in the 1 cup of cilantro and the chiles, soy sauce and lime juice. Season with salt, garnish with chopped cilantro and serve.

MAKE DIY BROWN SUGAR

It's late on a Saturday and you're craving chocolate chip cookies. You head to the pantry only to realize that you're completely out of brown sugar! If this has ever happened to you, I have an easy way for making sure it'll never happen again.

Combine 1 cup of granulated sugar and 1 tablespoon of unsulfured molasses in a food processor. Pulse until evenly colored. (For dark brown sugar, use 2 tablespoons of molasses.)

Pumpkin Muffins with Crumb Topping

Active **30 min**; Total **1 hr 15 min plus cooling**; Makes **12**

FILLING

⅓ **cup cream cheese, softened**

⅓ **cup confectioners' sugar**

1 **large egg yolk**

TOPPING

½ **cup all-purpose flour**

¼ **cup packed light brown sugar**

¾ **tsp. cinnamon**

¼ **tsp. kosher salt**

4 **Tbsp. cold unsalted butter, cubed**

MUFFINS

1½ **cups all-purpose flour**

1 **tsp. cinnamon**

Pinch of freshly grated nutmeg

Pinch of ground cloves

¾ **tsp. baking soda**

½ **tsp. baking powder**

½ **tsp. kosher salt**

2 **large eggs**

½ **cup packed light brown sugar**

½ **cup vegetable oil**

1 **cup canned pumpkin puree**

1. Make the filling In a small bowl, mix the cream cheese with the confectioners' sugar and egg yolk until creamy. Cover and freeze the filling until chilled, about 30 minutes.

2. Meanwhile, make the topping In a medium bowl, combine the flour, brown sugar, cinnamon and salt. Work in the butter with your fingers. Press the mixture into small clumps, then refrigerate the topping until chilled, about 15 minutes.

3. Make the muffins Preheat the oven to 350° and line a 12-cup muffin tin with paper or foil liners. In a medium bowl, whisk the flour with the cinnamon, nutmeg, cloves, baking soda, baking powder and salt. In a large bowl, using a hand mixer, beat the eggs with the brown sugar, oil and pumpkin puree at medium speed until combined. Beat in the dry ingredients until evenly incorporated.

4. Spoon half of the batter into the prepared muffin cups. Drop heaping teaspoons of the cream cheese filling in the center of each cup, then spoon the remaining batter on top. Sprinkle the crumb topping over the batter. Bake the muffins for about 30 minutes, until a toothpick inserted in the centers comes out clean. Let the muffins cool for 10 minutes before turning them out onto a rack to cool completely.

MAKE AHEAD The muffins can be stored in an airtight container at room temperature for up to 3 days.

CONTINUED ▶

▶ CONTINUED

MAKE DIY BROWN SUGAR

Glazed Agrodolce Ribs

Active **45 min**; Total **2 hr 45 min**; Serves **8**

I flavor these tender, juicy ribs with Tuscan seasonings—garlic, fennel seeds and fresh herbs—then quickly glaze them under the broiler with a sweet and tangy balsamic-laced barbecue sauce.

Two 4-lb. racks of pork spareribs, membranes removed

1½ Tbsp. fennel seeds, crushed

1½ Tbsp. finely chopped thyme

2 tsp. crushed red pepper

2 tsp. finely chopped rosemary

Kosher salt and black pepper

2 Tbsp. extra-virgin olive oil

1 small red onion, coarsely grated

3 garlic cloves, finely grated

1 cup balsamic vinegar

¼ cup distilled white vinegar

1 cup ketchup

¾ cup packed light brown sugar

1. Preheat the oven to 325°. Line 2 large rimmed baking sheets with foil and set the ribs on them, meaty side up. In a mortar, crush the fennel seeds with the thyme, crushed red pepper, chopped rosemary, 1½ tablespoons of salt and 2 teaspoons of black pepper. Rub the spice mix all over the ribs and roast for about 2 hours, until the meat is tender.

2. Meanwhile, in a medium saucepan, heat the olive oil. Add the onion, garlic and a generous pinch of salt and cook over moderately high heat, stirring, until the onion is softened, 3 to 5 minutes. Add both vinegars along with the ketchup and brown sugar and bring to a boil. Simmer over moderate heat, stirring frequently, until the sauce is thick and reduced to 2 cups, about 15 minutes.

3. Remove the ribs from the oven and turn on the broiler. Brush the underside of the racks with some of the sauce. Broil 1 sheet of ribs 8 inches from the heat until browned. Flip the ribs and repeat on the other side. Move the ribs to the bottom rack of the oven to keep warm while you glaze the rest.

4. Transfer the racks to a work surface. Cut in between the bones to form individual ribs and mound on a platter. Pass the remaining sauce at the table.

MAKE AHEAD The sauce can be refrigerated for up to 1 week.

Roasted Pork Loin with Cranberry-Apricot Chutney

Active **30 min**; Total **1 hr 30 min**
Serves **6 to 8**

2 Tbsp. vegetable oil

1 large shallot, finely chopped

1 garlic clove, minced

½ tsp. cinnamon

¼ tsp. ground cloves

Pinch of freshly grated nutmeg

1 lb. fresh or frozen cranberries

¾ cup dried apricots, finely chopped

¾ cup packed dark brown sugar

¼ cup apple cider vinegar

2 tsp. fresh lemon juice

Kosher salt and pepper

One 3½-lb. boneless pork loin roast, tied

1. In a medium saucepan, heat the oil. Add the shallot and garlic and cook over moderately high heat until softened, 3 minutes. Add the spices and cook for 2 minutes. Add the cranberries, apricots, sugar, vinegar and ¼ cup of water and cook, stirring, until the cranberries start to burst, 5 minutes. Mash some of the cranberries and cook, stirring, until thickened, 5 minutes. Stir in the lemon juice; season with salt and pepper. Let cool.

2. Meanwhile, preheat the oven to 450°. In a small roasting pan, season the pork generously with salt and pepper and roast for 20 minutes, until lightly browned. Reduce the oven temperature to 400° and roast for about 30 minutes longer, until an instant-read thermometer inserted in the thickest part of the meat registers 135°. Transfer the pork to a carving board and let rest for 15 minutes. Discard the strings. Thinly slice the pork and serve with the chutney.

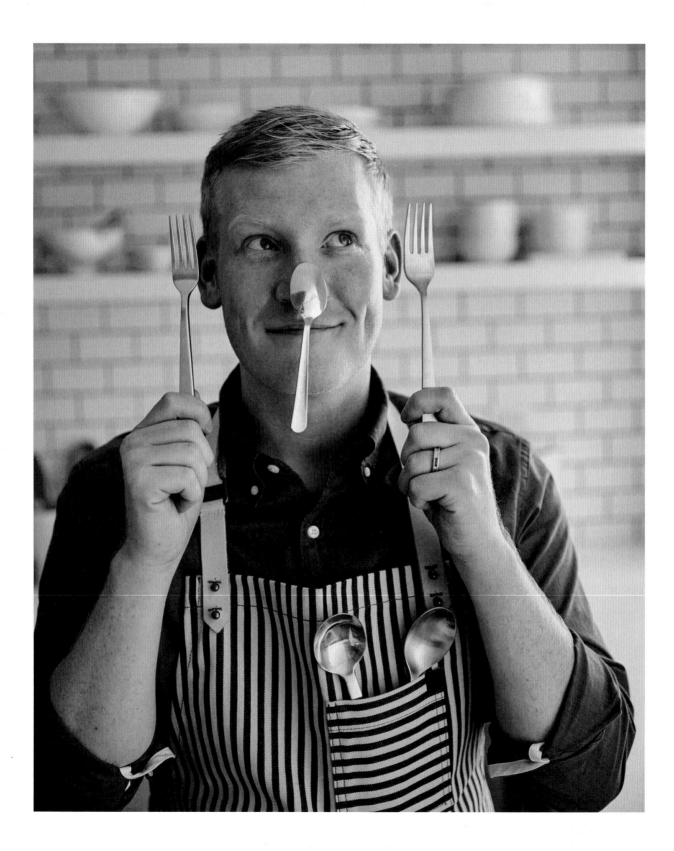

FORK+ SPOON

SEED POMEGRANATES

I love the pop of pomegranate seeds in winter salads and relishes, or to just eat on their own. Not only do they sparkle like jewels, they're packed with good-for-you antioxidants. The problem: The seeds are a real pain to remove from the pith. But my spoon hack gets all the pomegranate seeds out with almost no work at all.

 Hold one half of a pomegranate cut side down in your palm over a bowl of water. Tap the outside of the pomegranate all over with a wooden spoon to release the seeds into the water. Pour off the water and any pith before using the seeds.

Grilled Lamb Loin Chops with Pomegranate Relish

Total **30 min**; Serves **4 to 6**

> Eight 7- to 8-oz. lamb loin chops, cut 2 inches thick
>
> Kosher salt and pepper

1½ cups pomegranate seeds (from 2 pomegranates)

1 cup lightly packed mint, chopped, plus whole leaves for garnish

1 shallot, minced

3 Tbsp. extra-virgin olive oil

2 Tbsp. sherry vinegar

1. Light a grill or heat a cast-iron grill pan. Season the lamb chops with salt and pepper and grill over moderate heat, turning occasionally, until lightly charred all over and an instant-read thermometer inserted in the thickest part of the chops registers 130°, about 15 minutes. Transfer to a platter and let rest for 5 minutes.

2. In a medium bowl, mix the pomegranate seeds with the chopped mint, shallot, olive oil and vinegar; season with salt and pepper. Garnish the lamb chops with mint leaves and serve with the relish.

more uses for pomegranate

GUACAMOLE Fold pomegranate seeds into guacamole. They give the guac a great crunch and subtle sweetness.

RICE PILAF Mix fragrant basmati rice with pomegranate seeds, herbs and lime juice and serve alongside chicken or fish.

POMEGRANATE ROYALES Lightly muddle pomegranate seeds in Champagne flutes. Top with chilled sparkling wine or apple cider.

PEEL BOILED EGGS

STEP 1 Tap the wide end of a boiled egg on a work surface and peel off just the bottom of the shell.

STEP 2 Gently slide a small metal spoon between the shell and the egg white.

STEP 3 Rotate the egg until the shell is removed.

1

2

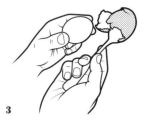

3

Deviled Eggs with Pickled Mustard Seeds

Total **30 min** plus cooling
Makes **12**

PICKLED MUSTARD SEEDS

¾ cup distilled white vinegar

¼ cup water

¼ cup yellow mustard seeds

1 Tbsp. sugar

1 garlic clove, lightly crushed

2 tsp. kosher salt

EGGS

6 large eggs

3 Tbsp. mayonnaise

1 tsp. Dijon mustard

1 tsp. distilled white vinegar

Kosher salt and pepper

Snipped chives, for garnish

1. Pickle the mustard seeds
In a small saucepan, combine all of the ingredients and bring to a boil. Simmer over moderate heat, stirring occasionally, until the seeds are tender and the liquid is reduced, about 20 minutes. Let cool completely.

2. Meanwhile, prepare the eggs
In a medium saucepan, cover the eggs with water. Bring to a boil, then simmer over moderate heat for 8 minutes. Drain and cool under running water, then peel the eggs and pat them dry.

3. Cut the eggs in half lengthwise and carefully scoop the yolks into a medium bowl; mash them with a fork. Stir in the mayonnaise, mustard, vinegar and 1½ tablespoons of the pickled mustard seeds. Season the filling with salt and pepper.

4. Arrange the egg whites on a platter. Spoon the filling into the egg whites and garnish with pickled mustard seeds and snipped chives. Serve.

MAKE AHEAD The pickled mustard seeds can be refrigerated for up to 2 weeks.

GRATE GINGER

Take a look at a fresh hand of ginger and you'll see it's covered with knobs and little nooks and crannies. That's what makes ginger so difficult to peel and grate. My solution: Remove the skin with a teaspoon! It's the perfect tool for getting into the crevices. Then you can grate that beautifully clean peeled ginger with the tines of a fork.

 STEP 1 Hold a piece of ginger in one hand and scrape off the skin with a spoon.

STEP 2 Hold a fork firmly on a work surface with the tines facing up. Scrape a knob of peeled ginger on the tines to grate it. Discard any stringy bits.

Sesame-Ginger Chicken Meatballs

Total **30 min;** Serves **4**

- Canola oil, for brushing
- 1 **lb. ground chicken, preferably dark meat**
- ½ **cup plain dry bread crumbs**
- ⅓ **cup minced scallions, plus thinly sliced scallions for garnish**
- 3 **Tbsp. grated peeled fresh ginger**
- 1 **large egg**
- 2 **garlic cloves, minced**
- 2 **tsp. toasted sesame oil**
- 2 **tsp. soy sauce**
- ¼ **tsp. kosher salt**
- **Asian chili sauce, for serving**

Preheat the oven to 450° and brush a rimmed baking sheet with canola oil. In a large bowl, mix together all of the remaining ingredients except the sliced scallions and chili sauce. Form the chicken mixture into 1½-inch balls and arrange them on the baking sheet. Brush the meatballs with canola oil and bake them for about 13 minutes, until they are browned and cooked through. Transfer the meatballs to a platter, garnish with sliced scallions and serve with chili sauce.

PREP KIWI

Peeling kiwi with a knife wastes a lot of fruit. A better, easier way is to use a spoon. You'll also wind up with a smoother surface, which in turn creates prettier slices.

STEP 1 Using a paring knife, cut off just the very end of a kiwi. Gently slide a small metal spoon between the flesh and the skin.

STEP 2 Slowly rotate the kiwi until the skin is separated from the fruit.

STEP 3 Squeeze out the fruit and discard the skin.

Kiwi Tartlets

Active **15 min**; Total **1 hr plus cooling**
Serves **6**

> One 14-oz. sheet of all-butter puff pastry
>
> ¼ cup sugar
>
> 1 cup fromage blanc or Greek yogurt
>
> ½ vanilla bean, split lengthwise and seeds scraped
>
> Pinch of kosher salt
>
> 2 Tbsp. agave nectar or honey, plus more for drizzling
>
> 3 ripe but firm kiwis, peeled and thinly sliced

1. Preheat the oven to 400°. Line a large rimmed baking sheet with parchment paper. On a lightly floured work surface, roll out the pastry to a 9-by-13-inch rectangle. Using a 4-inch round plate or plastic takeout lid as a template, cut out 6 rounds.

2. Transfer the pastry rounds to the lined baking sheet and poke them all over with a fork. Top with another sheet of parchment and another baking sheet and bake for about 20 minutes, until the pastry is lightly browned. Remove the top sheet and parchment paper and sprinkle with the sugar. Bake the rounds for about 20 minutes longer, until browned and crisp. Transfer the rounds to a rack and let cool completely.

3. In a small bowl, whisk the fromage blanc with the vanilla seeds, salt and the 2 tablespoons of agave. Spread the mixture on the tarts and top with the kiwi slices. Drizzle with agave and serve.

MAKE AHEAD The tart shells can be stored in an airtight container overnight.

STUFF GRILLED CHEESE

Food & Wine contributing editor Andrew Zimmern is a fearless eater. I can't pronounce half the things he eats on his Travel Channel show, *Bizarre Foods*, but he taught me this genius grilled cheese trick. You crimp the edges of the bread with a fork so it holds in all the oozy filling.

STEP 1 Cut the crusts off slices of white sandwich bread.

STEP 2 Spread half of the bread slices with the cheese filling, leaving a border.

STEP 3 Close the sandwiches and crimp the edges with a fork to seal them tightly.

Pimento Cheese–Stuffed Sandwiches

Total **45 min**; Serves **4**

- 4 oz. sharp yellow cheddar cheese, shredded (1 cup)
- ½ roasted red bell pepper, chopped
- 1 Tbsp. finely grated onion
- ¼ cup mayonnaise
  Kosher salt and pepper
- 8 slices of white sandwich bread, crusts removed
  Softened butter, for brushing

1. In a food processor, combine the cheddar cheese with the roasted bell pepper, onion and mayonnaise and pulse until the cheese and pepper are coarsely chopped. Season the pimento cheese with salt and pepper.

2. Spread 4 slices of bread each with 3 to 4 tablespoons of the pimento cheese, leaving a ½-inch border. Top with the remaining bread slices and, using a fork, crimp the edges of the sandwiches to seal them tightly. Refrigerate for 15 minutes.

3. Set a griddle over two burners and turn the heat to moderate. Butter both sides of the stuffed sandwiches. Griddle over moderate heat, turning once, until the sandwiches are lightly browned and the cheese is melted, about 4 minutes. Serve.

KNIFE

CORE ZUCCHINI

My method removes the watery core of the vegetable, leaving you with firm, flat pieces that will brown nicely. This technique also works for cucumbers and eggplant.

STEP 1 Cut your zucchini in two, then stand each half upright on a work surface.

STEP 2 Cut the zucchini off the seedy core, rotating the zucchini as you go. Discard the core.

STEP 3 Cut the zucchini slabs on the diagonal into 1-inch-thick pieces.

Sesame-Marinated Zucchini

Active **15 min**; Total **45 min**; Serves **4**

- 3 medium zucchini, trimmed and halved crosswise
- 1 Tbsp. canola oil
- 1 garlic clove, minced
- 2½ Tbsp. unseasoned rice vinegar
- 2 Tbsp. soy sauce
- 1 tsp. toasted sesame oil
- 1 tsp. toasted sesame seeds
- 2 scallions, thinly sliced on the diagonal

1. Hold a zucchini half upright on a work surface. Using a sharp knife, cut the zucchini off the round core in 4 or 5 pieces; discard the core. Cut the zucchini pieces on the diagonal 1 inch thick. Repeat with the remaining zucchini.

2. In a large cast-iron skillet, heat the canola oil. Add the zucchini pieces skin side up and cook over high heat until lightly charred on the bottom, about 2 minutes. Add the garlic and cook, stirring gently, until the zucchini is crisp-tender, about 1 minute longer. Transfer to a large bowl and let cool.

3. Add the vinegar, soy sauce and sesame oil and seeds to the zucchini and mix well. Cover and refrigerate for 30 minutes. Stir in the scallions and serve chilled or at room temperature.

MAKE AHEAD The marinated zucchini can be refrigerated overnight. Let stand at room temperature for 15 minutes before serving.

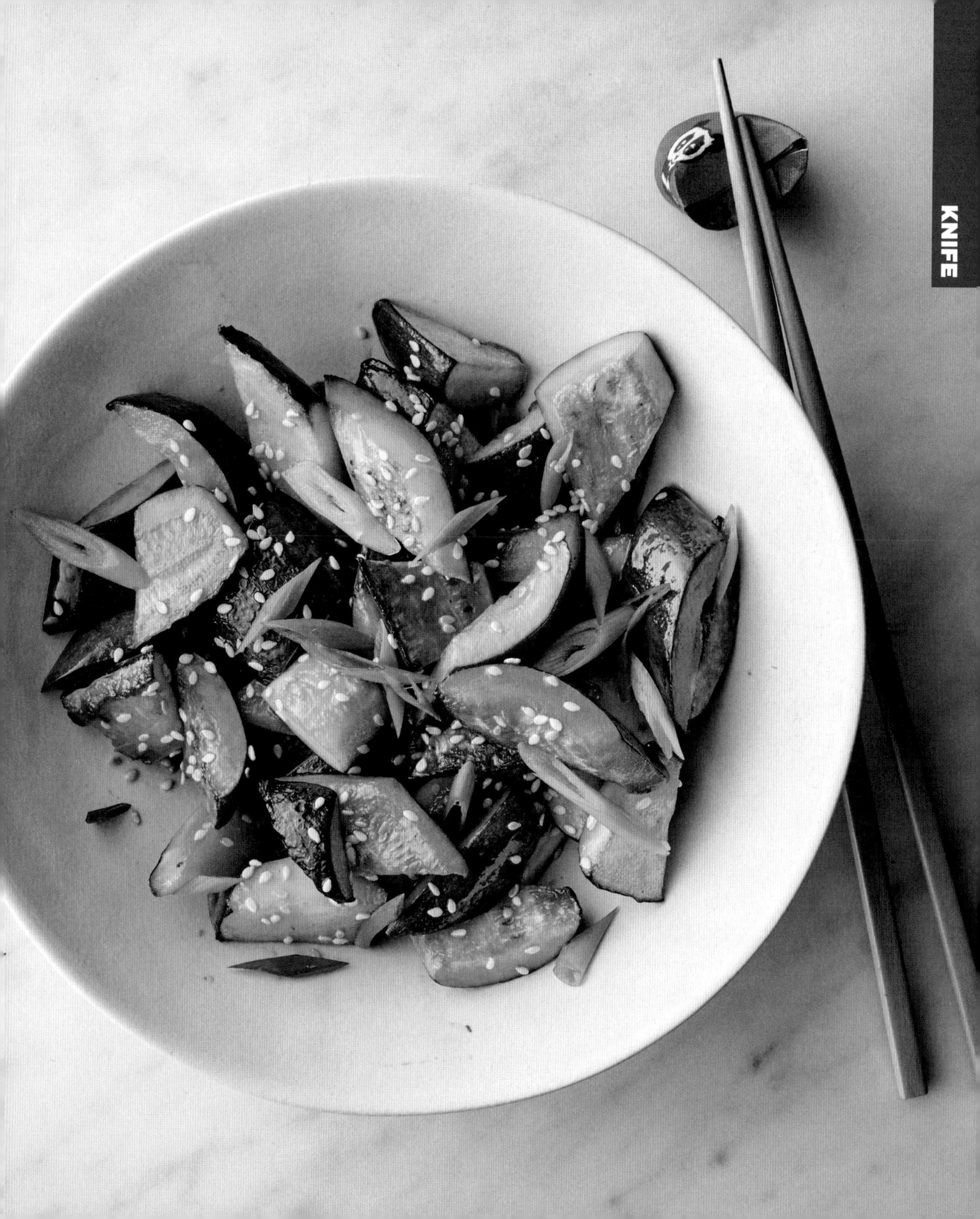

CUBE MELON

STEP 1 Start with a quarter wedge of watermelon. Using a large, sharp knife, make horizontal cuts down to the rind at 1-inch intervals—be sure to angle the knife so that it's parallel to the opposite flat surface of the wedge. Repeat on the other side.

STEP 2 Make even vertical cuts down to the rind along the entire wedge.

STEP 3 Scoop the cubes into a bowl. For a video, go to foodandwine.com/video/mad-genius-cooking-tips.

1

2

3

Watermelon and Chicken Salad with Hot Sauce Vinaigrette
Total **25 min**; Serves **4**

- One 3-lb. seedless watermelon wedge
- ½ lb. shredded cooked chicken (3 cups)
- 2 oz. arugula (not baby), chopped (4 cups)
- ½ cup chopped marcona almonds
- ⅓ cup snipped chives
- ¼ cup extra-virgin olive oil
- 3 Tbsp. fresh lemon juice
- 1 tsp. Tabasco or other Louisiana-style hot sauce
- Kosher salt and pepper

1. Cut the watermelon into cubes according to the directions at left. Scoop the cubes into a serving bowl, then add the chicken, arugula, almonds and chives.

2. In a small bowl, whisk the olive oil with the lemon juice and Tabasco and season with salt and pepper. Add to the serving bowl and gently toss to mix. Season with salt and pepper and toss again. Serve right away.

ROLL-CUT CARROTS

This tip allows you to cut a carrot into pieces that will cook evenly.

STEP 1 Slice one end of a carrot on the diagonal. Rotate it a quarter turn and make another slice.

STEP 2 Continue turning and slicing until you reach the end of the carrot.

STEP 3 Transfer the roll-cut carrots to a skillet and cook.

Cumin-and-Butter-Braised Carrots

Total **25 min**; Serves **4**

- 2 **large carrots (1 lb.), peeled and trimmed**
- 2 **Tbsp. extra-virgin olive oil**
- 2 **tsp. cumin seeds**
- ¼ **tsp. crushed red pepper**
  Kosher salt and black pepper
- ½ **cup chicken stock or low-sodium broth**
- 2 **Tbsp. unsalted butter**
- ¼ **cup chopped cilantro**
- 2 **tsp. distilled white vinegar**

1. Hold a carrot parallel to you on a work surface. Position a knife diagonally over the tapered end of the carrot and make a ¾-inch-wide slice. Rotate the carrot a quarter turn and make another ¾-inch-wide slice. Continue to rotate and slice the carrot until you reach the end.

2. In a large skillet, heat the oil. Add the cumin seeds and crushed red pepper and cook over moderately high heat, stirring, until fragrant, about 1 minute. Add the carrots and a generous pinch each of salt and black pepper and cook for 2 minutes, stirring occasionally. Add the stock and butter and bring to a boil. Cover and simmer over moderate heat until the carrots are crisp-tender, about 5 minutes. Uncover and simmer, stirring occasionally, until the carrots are glazed, 1 to 2 minutes longer. Stir in the cilantro and vinegar and season with salt and black pepper. Serve.

MAKE AHEAD The carrots can be refrigerated overnight. Reheat gently and stir in the cilantro and vinegar before serving.

FLATTEN PORK CHOPS AND STEAKS

A good pork chop has a nice fat cap that keeps it juicy. But the minute the meat hits a hot skillet, the fat tightens and makes the chop curl up—and you end up with more of a pork cup. My trick keeps your chop flat in the pan so it cooks evenly.

 Score the fat cap in ½-inch intervals just until the knife reaches the meat.

Coriander-Crusted Pork Chops with Jicama, Avocado and Apple Salad

Total **45 min; Serves 4**

The coriander-lime crust gives these pork chops great flavor inspired by Mexican cooking. They're fantastic with the crunchy, cooling salad on the side.

> **Four 10-oz. bone-in pork rib chops, fat scored**

2 **Tbsp. extra-virgin olive oil, plus more for brushing**

1 **Tbsp. coriander seeds, crushed**

1½ **tsp. finely grated lime zest**

> **Kosher salt and pepper**

½ **lb. jicama, peeled and cut into ½-inch pieces**

1 **Granny Smith apple—halved, cored and julienned**

1 **large Hass avocado—peeled, pitted and cut into 1-inch pieces**

½ **cup lightly packed cilantro, chopped**

3 **Tbsp. fresh lime juice**

1. Preheat the oven to 400°. Preheat a large cast-iron skillet over moderately high heat. Brush the pork chops with olive oil and sprinkle all over with the coriander seeds and lime zest; season with salt and pepper. Add the pork chops to the skillet and cook over moderately high heat, turning once, until well browned, about 8 minutes. Transfer the skillet to the oven and roast until an instant-read thermometer inserted in the thickest part of the pork registers 135°, about 7 minutes. Transfer to plates and let rest for 5 minutes.

2. Meanwhile, in a large bowl, toss the jicama with the apple, avocado, cilantro, lime juice and the 2 tablespoons of olive oil. Season with salt and pepper. Pile the salad alongside the pork chops and serve right away.

VARIATION Combine brown sugar with paprika, chili powder, garlic powder and dried oregano. Rub on pork and let stand for 15 minutes at room temperature.

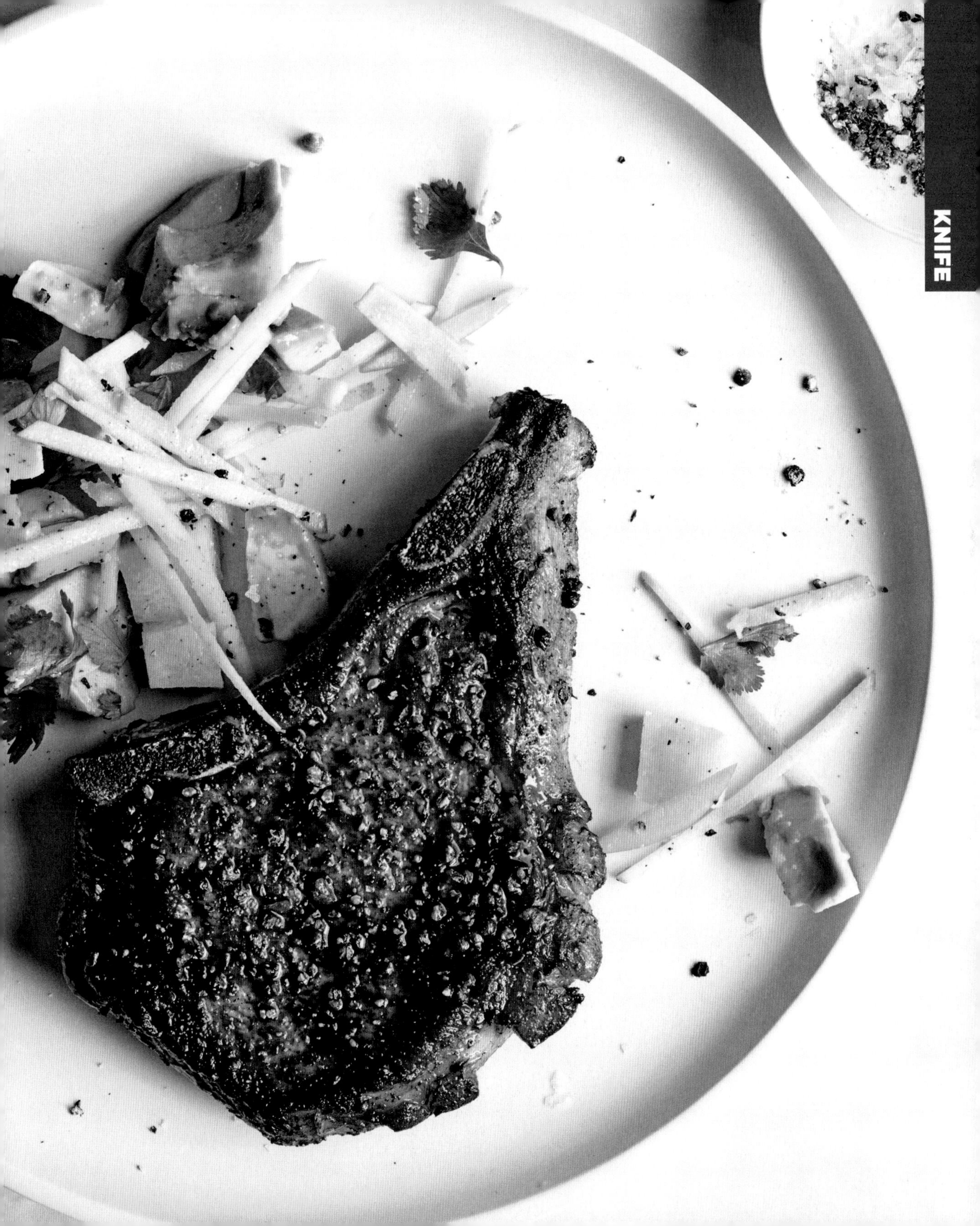

TRUSSING SHORTCUT

If you don't have kitchen twine on hand, you can still truss a chicken or turkey with my simple trick.

 STEP 1 Make a slit with a knife in one side of the excess chicken skin around the cavity.

STEP 2 Carefully slip the end of the drumstick from the opposite side into the slit.

STEP 3 Repeat on the other side with the remaining drumstick.

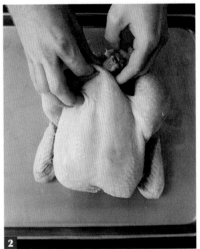

Roast Chicken Paprikash with Watercress and Dilled Sour Cream

Active **35 min**; Total **1 hr 20 min**
Serves **4**

    One 3½-lb. whole chicken
 2 Tbsp. extra-virgin olive oil
 2 tsp. sweet paprika
 2 tsp. hot paprika
 2 tsp. caraway seeds
 2 small garlic cloves, finely grated
    Kosher salt and pepper
 ½ cup sour cream
 2 Tbsp. minced dill
 4 oz. watercress
 1 Tbsp. fresh lemon juice

1. Preheat the oven to 425°. Using a small, sharp knife, make a ¾-inch slit in one side of the excess chicken skin around the cavity; carefully slip the end of the drumstick from the opposite side into the slit. Repeat on the other side with the remaining drumstick.

2. In a small bowl, whisk 1 tablespoon of the olive oil with the sweet paprika, hot paprika, caraway seeds, garlic, 1 tablespoon of salt and ½ teaspoon of pepper. Set the chicken in a small roasting pan and rub all over with the mixture. Roast the chicken for about 45 minutes, until an instant-read thermometer inserted in an inner thigh registers 165°. Transfer the chicken to a carving board and let rest for 15 minutes.

3. Meanwhile, in another small bowl, whisk the sour cream with the dill and season with salt and pepper. On a platter, toss the watercress with the lemon juice and the remaining 1 tablespoon of olive oil and season with salt and pepper.

4. Carve the chicken and arrange the pieces on the watercress. Drizzle any pan juices over the chicken and serve right away, with the dilled sour cream.

MAKE ICE CREAM SLABS

POPS

Everything tastes better on a stick, including ice cream! Insert sticks into the slabs, then dip them in chocolate. Finish with a dusting of sprinkles or pearled sugar.

The super-easy recipes that follow all feature ice cream slabs that you slice from a cardboard pint.

 With a large serrated knife, cut pint containers of firm ice cream into ¾-inch-thick rounds. Cut a slit in the cardboard, then peel off.

Chocolate Shell Pops

Total **15 min;** Makes **2 cups chocolate, enough for about 8 pops**

This is my upgraded version of Magic Shell, the sauce that quickly hardens when poured over cold things. Coconut oil adds a ton of extra flavor.

- 1 **lb. bittersweet chocolate, finely chopped**
- ½ **cup coconut oil**
  Kosher salt
  Ice cream slabs, each stuck with a popsicle stick

In a large microwave-safe bowl, melt the chopped chocolate with the coconut oil at high power in 20-second bursts, stirring between intervals. Stir in a generous pinch of salt and let stand at room temperature until cooled before coating ice cream pops.

CONTINUED ▶

▶ CONTINUED

MAKE ICE CREAM SLABS

SANDWICHES

Set slices of ice cream between cookies for superquick sandwiches. Take them to the next level by dipping them in melted chocolate or rolling them in chopped nuts–or both! Here are a few of my favorite combinations: green tea ice cream sandwiches dipped in chocolate, and cherry ice cream sandwiches rolled in pistachios or dipped in chocolate.

TERRINE

You can arrange slabs of different ice creams and sorbets in a loaf pan to create the easiest terrine ever. For the most visual impact, I stack flavors in contrasting colors, which create cool swirled scoops! Here, from top to bottom: raspberry sorbet, chocolate, strawberry, green tea and vanilla ice cream.

MASON JAR

MAKE OVERNIGHT OATS

We all know that breakfast is the most important meal of the day. I love to eat something healthy, like oatmeal. But who on earth has time to make it in the morning? Read on for a trick to prep a no-cook oatmeal that's ready when you wake up.

 Combine oatmeal ingredients in a Mason jar. Shake, then refrigerate overnight.

PB&J Overnight Oats

Total **10 min plus overnight soaking**
Serves **1**

This oatmeal is a healthy way to satisfy your PB&J cravings. I flavor the oats with peanut butter, then swirl in strawberry jam when I'm ready to eat, but feel free to use your favorite jam or jelly.

¾   **cup unsweetened almond milk**

2   **Tbsp. creamy peanut butter**

2   **tsp. honey**

2   **tsp. chia seeds**

2   **tsp. flax seeds**

¼   **tsp. kosher salt**

½   **cup old-fashioned rolled oats**

    Strawberry jam and coarsely chopped peanuts, for serving

In a 1-pint Mason jar, combine the almond milk with the peanut butter, honey, chia and flax seeds and the salt. Close the jar and shake until well combined. Add the oats, close the jar and shake again. Refrigerate overnight. Serve with strawberry jam and coarsely chopped peanuts.

ingredient swaps

MILK In place of the almond milk, swap in another nut milk, such as cashew or hazelnut, or use soy milk or regular milk.

NUT BUTTER Instead of peanut butter, use almond butter, then garnish with sliced almonds instead of peanuts. Or try Nutella with chopped hazelnuts. May not be as healthy, but it's so good!

JUICE Instead of milk, add a fruit juice, like apple. Omit the honey if you go this route.

SPICES Shake up your oats with ground cinnamon. Then garnish with apple chips and sliced almonds.

DIY A NOODLE CUP

 STEP 1 Make a fast and easy broth base in a Mason jar with miso, soy sauce and water.

STEP 2 Add ramen noodles.

STEP 3 Top the ramen with your favorite soup ingredients.

STEP 4 When you're ready to eat, fill the jar with boiling water, cover and let stand for 5 minutes.

Miso Chicken Noodle Cup
Total **15 min**; Serves **1**

- 2 Tbsp. shiro (white) miso
- 2 tsp. soy sauce
- 1¾ oz. ramen noodles, broken into smaller pieces
- ⅓ cup shredded cooked chicken
- ¼ cup baby spinach
- 1 large shiitake mushroom, stem discarded, cap very thinly sliced
- 1 slice of lime

In a 1-pint Mason jar, whisk the miso with the soy sauce and 2 teaspoons of water. Add the remaining ingredients. To serve, fill the jar with boiling water, cover and let stand for 5 minutes. Shake lightly before serving.

MAKE AHEAD The noodle cup can be assembled and refrigerated overnight. Add boiling water before serving.

PACK A PORTABLE SALAD

This salad is so pretty, but let me tell you why assembling it in a Mason jar is also really smart: The container is likely to stay upright in your bag, and even if it does tip over, it's sealed tightly so the dressing won't leak all over. Plus, by layering the ingredients the way I do, the cabbage marinates in the dressing while the more delicate ingredients stay fresh.

Pour dressing into the Mason jar first. Layer salad ingredients with the heaviest ones on the bottom.

Pickled Cabbage Salad with Chicken

Active **30 min**; Total **1 hr 30 min**; Serves **4**

- 1 cup distilled white vinegar
- 3 Tbsp. packed light brown sugar
  Kosher salt and pepper
- ½ lb. red cabbage, shredded
- 1 large carrot, shredded (1 cup)
- 1 Fresno chile—halved, seeded and thinly sliced
- ½ lb. green cabbage, shredded
- 1 Tbsp. Asian fish sauce
- 2½ Tbsp. extra-virgin olive oil
- 3 cups shredded cooked chicken (12 oz.)
- 1 cup cilantro leaves
- ½ cup coarsely chopped honey-roasted peanuts

1. In a medium bowl, whisk the vinegar and 1 cup of water with the sugar and 1 tablespoon of salt. Pour half of the brine into another medium bowl. Add the red cabbage to one bowl along with half of the carrot and chile. Add the green cabbage to the other bowl along with the remaining carrot and chile. Refrigerate the cabbages until pickled, about 1 hour.

2. Drain the cabbages, reserving ¼ cup of the brine from the green cabbage. In a small bowl, whisk the reserved brine with the fish sauce and olive oil and season with salt and pepper. Divide the dressing among four 1-pint Mason jars, then layer in the red and green cabbages, followed by the chicken. Top with the cilantro and peanuts and serve.

MAKE AHEAD The salad can be refrigerated overnight.

VARIATION Use solid white tuna, poached salmon or diced tofu in place of the shredded cooked chicken.

SHAKE COCKTAILS

Mixing drinks in individual Mason jars is great for parties because it lets your guests join in on the fun. Plus, it means you don't have to keep rinsing out your one and only cocktail shaker between drinks.

 Combine cocktail ingredients in a Mason jar. Fill with ice cubes, close the jar and shake well.

Cucumber and Mint "Fauxjito"

Total **5 min;** Makes **1**

My virgin riff on a classic mojito is incredibly refreshing. Packed with fresh mint and topped with club soda, it has a cooling quality from cucumber and a hint of sweetness from agave.

- 6 **thin slices of English cucumber, plus 1 long, thin slice for garnish**
- 6 **large mint leaves, plus 1 sprig for garnish**
- 2 **oz. fresh lime juice**
- ½ **oz. agave nectar**
  Ice
- 4 **oz. chilled club soda**

In a 1-pint Mason jar, muddle the 6 cucumber slices with the mint leaves. Add the lime juice and agave nectar; fill with ice. Close the jar and shake well. Strain into an ice-filled collins glass. Top with the soda; stir once. Garnish with the long cucumber slice and mint sprig.

Mixed-Berry Martini

Total **5 min;** Makes **1**

This tart, fruity cocktail is best in the summer when berries are at their peak. People always go crazy for the color and immediately want to try the drink.

- 5 **raspberries**
- 2 **Tbsp. blueberries, plus 1 for garnish**
- 3 **blackberries**
- 2 **oz. vodka**
- 1½ **oz. fresh lime juice**
  Ice

In a 1-pint Mason jar, muddle 4 of the raspberries with the 2 tablespoons of blueberries and 2 of the blackberries. Stir in the vodka and lime juice and fill with ice. Close the jar and shake well. Strain the cocktail into a chilled coupe. Skewer the remaining raspberry, blueberry and blackberry on a pick, garnish the cocktail and serve.

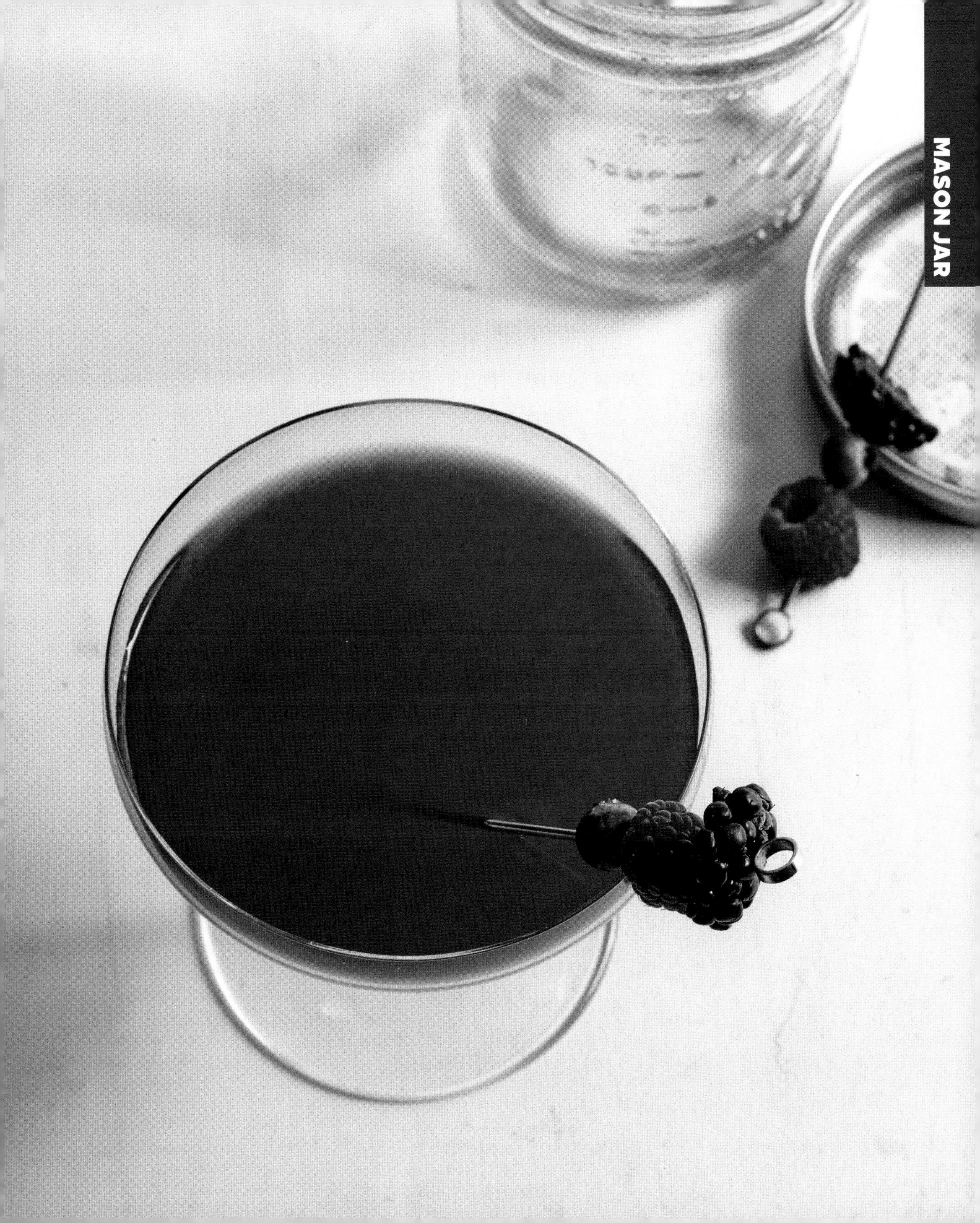

MICROWAVE

MAKE CHEESE SNACKS

Several years ago, I requested a small wedge of Parmigiano-Reggiano for a grocery order for the *Food & Wine* Test Kitchen. What arrived was as big as a cinder block! Instead of letting the excess cheese just sit in the fridge, I came up with these quick, delicious snacks that are perfect for a last-minute party.

 Zap Parmigiano-Reggiano cheese in the microwave and you'll get crisp, irresistible snacks in a fraction of the time it would take on the stove or in the oven.

Thyme and Black Pepper Frico

📷 OPPOSITE

Total **10 min**; Makes **8**

Frico are lacy, thin Italian cheese crisps that are awesome with cocktails. You usually melt them in a skillet, but they can burn easily. My cheater's version is foolproof.

- **½ cup finely grated Parmigiano-Reggiano cheese**
- **2 tsp. chopped thyme**
- **1 tsp. coarsely ground black pepper**

In a small bowl, mix the Parmesan with the thyme and pepper. Spoon 1 tablespoon of the mixture on a small microwave-safe plate and gently shake the plate to form a 3-inch round of cheese. Microwave at high power for 45 to 60 seconds, until the cheese is melted and lacy. Using an offset spatula, transfer to a rack to cool. Repeat with the remaining cheese mixture. Serve.

MAKE AHEAD The frico can be stored in an airtight container overnight, but not on a humid day!

Parmigiano-Reggiano Puffs

Total **5 min**

Top Chef judge Richard Blais shared this amazing trick with me. You take leftover Parmesan rinds (keep them in the freezer and pull them out when you're ready) and microwave them until they puff up. I serve them at parties, and guests can't believe that these supercrispy cheese puffs were once Parmesan rinds! They're also terrific on top of a salad.

Parmigiano-Reggiano cheese rinds, cut into ½-inch dice

On a microwave-safe plate, microwave the cheese rinds at high power until puffed and sizzling, 30 seconds to 1 minute. Transfer the cheese puffs to paper towels to drain. Serve hot.

DRY HERBS

I hate letting my summer herb crop go to waste, so I dry fresh sprigs quickly in the microwave to extend their shelf life. The most zappable herbs are sturdy ones like rosemary, thyme and oregano. After the herbs are dried, just run your fingers along the sprigs to strip off the leaves. Discard the stems and store the dried herbs in spice jars.

STEP 1 Arrange sprigs of fresh herbs on a paper towel so they don't touch each other.

STEP 2 Microwave at high power in 20-second bursts until the herbs are dried and crisp; turn and flip them between intervals.

STEP 3 Strip the dried leaves from the stems.

Grilled Swordfish with Dried Herbs and Charred Lemon Salsa

Total **50 min**; Serves **4**

Swordfish is so meaty and flavorful, it's like the steak of the sea. The fish is hearty enough to stand up to assertive ingredients like the dried rosemary, thyme and oregano here.

- 1 lemon, preferably thin-skinned, very thinly sliced and seeded
- ¼ cup extra-virgin olive oil, plus more for brushing
- 1 medium celery rib, finely chopped
- 2 Tbsp. minced shallot
- ¼ cup finely chopped parsley
- 2 tsp. each dried rosemary, thyme and oregano

  Kosher salt and pepper

  Four 8-oz. skinless swordfish steaks, cut 1 inch thick

1. Light a grill or heat a grill pan. Brush the lemon slices with olive oil and grill over moderate heat, turning occasionally, until lightly charred and the rind is tender, about 8 minutes. Transfer to a work surface, let cool, then finely chop.

2. In a small bowl, whisk the chopped lemon with the celery, shallot, parsley, ¼ cup of olive oil and ½ teaspoon each of the rosemary, thyme and oregano. Season the salsa with salt and pepper.

3. Brush the swordfish with olive oil and season with salt, pepper and the remaining 1½ teaspoons each of dried herbs. Grill the fish over moderately high heat, turning once, until lightly charred and just cooked through, 8 minutes. Transfer to plates and serve with the salsa.

SERVE WITH Sautéed greens.

CONTINUED ▶

DRY HERBS

Herb-Crusted Pork Chops

Total **30 min**; Serves **4**

- 2 tsp. ground fennel
- 2 tsp. each dried thyme and oregano
- 1 tsp. dried rosemary
- ½ tsp. finely grated lemon zest
- Four 10-oz. pork rib chops
- Extra-virgin olive oil, for brushing
- Kosher salt and pepper
- Lemon wedges, for serving

1. Light a grill or heat a grill pan. In a small bowl, mix all of the herbs with the lemon zest. Brush the pork chops all over with olive oil and rub with the herb mixture. Season generously with salt and pepper.

2. Grill the pork over moderate heat, turning occasionally, until lightly charred and an instant-read thermometer inserted in each chop near the bone registers 135°, about 13 minutes. Transfer to a platter and let rest for 5 minutes. Serve with lemon wedges.

Whole-Wheat Rosemary Crisps

Active **30 min**; Total **2 hr**; Makes **two 12-inch rounds**

- 2 chicken bouillon cubes (about ½ oz. each)
- ⅓ cup hot water
- ¾ cup all-purpose flour, plus more for dusting
- ½ cup whole-wheat flour
- 1½ tsp. sugar
- ½ tsp. kosher salt
- 4 Tbsp. cold unsalted butter
- Milk, for brushing
- Crushed dried rosemary leaves, for sprinkling

1. In a small bowl, dissolve 1 of the bouillon cubes in the hot water. Let the broth cool completely, then refrigerate until chilled, about 15 minutes.

2. In a food processor, pulse both flours with the sugar and salt. Scatter the butter on top and pulse until a coarse meal forms. Add the broth and pulse until the dough comes together. Transfer to a work surface and gather into a ball. Cut in half and pat into disks; wrap in plastic and refrigerate for 1 hour.

3. Preheat the oven to 400°. Line 2 baking sheets with parchment paper. On a lightly floured work surface, roll out each disk of dough to a 12-inch round and transfer to a prepared baking sheet. Brush the rounds with milk and sprinkle with rosemary. Finely grate the second bouillon cube on top.

4. Bake the crackers for about 18 minutes, until crisp. Let cool completely, then break into large shards and serve.

MAKE AHEAD The crisps can be stored in an airtight container for up to 1 week.

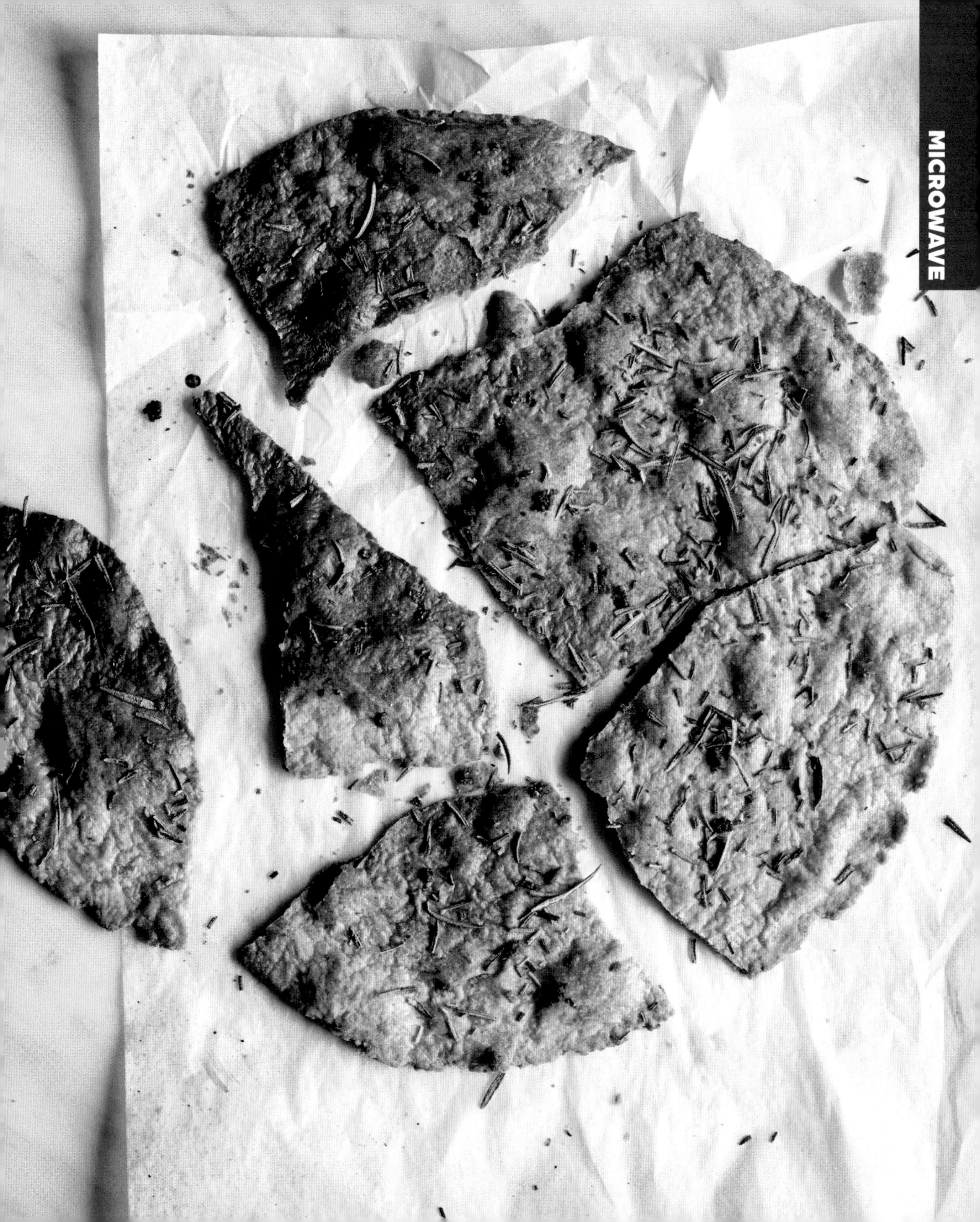

SOFTEN BROWN SUGAR

You're super-excited to bake your favorite treat. So you head to the pantry and grab that box of brown sugar. Then the nightmare happens: The sugar is rock hard! Fear not, because I have a tip to soften it up in no time flat.

Put clumps of hard brown sugar in a large microwave-safe bowl. Cover the sugar with a damp paper towel and zap at high power in 20-second bursts until fluffy; stir the sugar with a fork between intervals.

Pear and Sour Cream Coffee Cake

Active **50 min**; Total **2 hr plus cooling**
Serves **12**

TOPPING

- 1½ **cups all-purpose flour**
- 1 **cup rolled oats**
- 1 **cup pecans, coarsely chopped (optional)**
- 1 **cup light brown sugar**
- 2½ **tsp. cinnamon**
- 1 **tsp. ground ginger**
- 1 **tsp. kosher salt**
- 1 **stick plus 6 Tbsp. unsalted butter, softened**
- 2 **Bartlett pears—peeled, cored and cut into ½-inch pieces**

CAKE

- 2 **sticks unsalted butter, softened, plus more for greasing**
- 2½ **cups all-purpose flour**
- 1 **tsp. baking powder**
- ¾ **tsp. baking soda**
- 1 **tsp. kosher salt**
- 1½ **cups granulated sugar**
- 3 **large eggs**
- 1¼ **cups sour cream**
- 2 **tsp. pure vanilla extract**
  Confectioners' sugar, for dusting (optional)

1. Make the topping In a large bowl, whisk the flour with the oats, pecans (if using), brown sugar, cinnamon, ginger and salt. With your hands, rub the butter into the mixture until incorporated, pressing it into clumps. Add the pears and toss well. Refrigerate the topping until chilled, about 20 minutes.

2. Meanwhile, make the cake Preheat the oven to 350° and grease a 9-by-13-inch metal baking pan. In a medium bowl, whisk the flour, baking powder, baking soda and salt. In a stand mixer fitted with the paddle, beat the 2 sticks of butter with the granulated sugar at medium speed until fluffy, about 2 minutes. Beat in the eggs one at a time, then beat in the sour cream and vanilla. Scrape down the side of the bowl, then beat the dry ingredients into the batter in three additions until just incorporated.

3. Scrape the batter into the prepared pan, spreading it in an even layer. Cover with the streusel-pear topping. Bake for 1 hour and 15 minutes, until the crumb topping is browned and a toothpick inserted in the center of the cake comes out clean. Transfer the pan to a rack and let the cake cool completely, about 1 hour. Dust the cake with confectioners' sugar, cut into squares and serve.

BAKE A MUG CAKE

My friend Kristen Kish, *Top Chef* Season 10 winner, inspired this super-easy dessert. It's perfect for those days when you're in the mood for cake but don't want (or can't wait) to bake a whole one. With just a few ingredients, you can make an almost-instant mini cake.

 Mix cake batter ingredients in a mug. Microwave on high until the cake rises.

Chocolate Pudding Cake with Caramel Sauce

Total **5 min**; Serves **1**

This individual pudding cake has a fluffy exterior surrounding a gooey center, almost like molten chocolate cake.

- 2 **Tbsp. unsalted butter**
- ½ **cup buttermilk**
- 3 **Tbsp. sugar**
- 1 **large egg**
- ¼ **tsp. pure vanilla extract**
   Flaky sea salt, such as Maldon
- ⅓ **cup all-purpose flour**
- 2 **Tbsp. unsweetened cocoa powder**
- ½ **tsp. baking powder**
   Caramel sauce, for serving

In a large microwave-safe mug, melt the butter. Whisk in the buttermilk, sugar, egg, vanilla and a pinch of sea salt. Whisk in the flour, cocoa powder and baking powder until smooth. Microwave at high power for 60 to 90 seconds, until the cake has risen; do not let it overflow. Let cool slightly, then drizzle with caramel sauce and sprinkle with salt. Serve.

almost-instant rice pudding

This recipe is a fabulous way to use leftover rice, but you might love it so much that you always make extra rice for it.

Rice Pudding in a Mug
In a large mug, whisk together ¼ cup **whole milk**, 2 Tbsp. **sugar**, 1 Tbsp. **heavy cream**, ¼ tsp. **cinnamon**, ⅛ tsp. **pure vanilla extract** and a pinch of **kosher salt**. Stir in ¾ cup **cooked white rice** and 2 Tbsp. **raisins**. Microwave at high power in 30-second bursts until thickened slightly, 1½ to 2½ minutes. Stir between intervals. Let stand for 2 minutes, then garnish with more **raisins** and **toasted sliced almonds** before serving. *Serves 1.*

MUFFIN PAN

SHAPE CRAB CAKES

Anyone who loves crab cakes knows that the best ones have very little filler. But that also makes it difficult for them to hold their shape. With my muffin pan hack, not one crab cake will fall apart!

 Lightly pack the crabmeat mixture into muffin pan cups, then freeze until the cakes are barely firm.

Scallion Crab Cakes with Sesame Mayo
Active **25 min**; Total **1 hr**; Serves **4**

- ¾ cup mayonnaise
- 1½ cups panko
- ½ cup thinly sliced scallions
- 1 tsp. finely grated lime zest
- 1 Tbsp. plus 2 tsp. fresh lime juice
     Kosher salt and pepper
- 1 lb. jumbo lump crabmeat, picked over
- ¾ tsp. toasted sesame oil
- ½ tsp. Sriracha
- 1 large egg
- 6 Tbsp. extra-virgin olive oil

1. In a large bowl, whisk ¼ cup of the mayonnaise with ½ cup of the panko and the scallions, lime zest, 1 tablespoon of the lime juice, 1 teaspoon of salt and ½ teaspoon of pepper. Fold in the crab. Lightly pack the crab mixture into the cups of a 12-cup muffin pan. Freeze until the cakes are barely firm, about 30 minutes.

2. Meanwhile, preheat the oven to 375°. In a small bowl, whisk the remaining ½ cup of mayonnaise and 2 teaspoons of lime juice with the sesame oil and Sriracha. Season the sesame mayo with salt and pepper.

3. Invert the crab cakes onto a large baking sheet. In a shallow bowl, beat the egg. Spread the remaining 1 cup of panko in another shallow bowl. Dip the crab cakes in the egg and then dredge in the panko, pressing lightly to help it adhere.

4. In a large nonstick skillet, heat 3 tablespoons of the olive oil until shimmering. Add 6 of the crab cakes and cook over moderately high heat, turning once, until golden, about 4 minutes; return them to the baking sheet. Repeat with the remaining 3 tablespoons of oil and 6 crab cakes.

5. Bake the crab cakes until heated through, about 5 minutes. Serve with the sesame mayo.

MAKE AHEAD The crab cakes can be prepared through Step 1 and frozen for up to 1 week. Let the cakes thaw for 30 minutes before proceeding.

POACH EGGS

Pour a little water into the cups of a muffin pan. Crack an egg into each cup and bake until the whites are just firm and the yolks are still runny.

FARBERWARE®

CONTINUED ▶

POACH EGGS

Open-Face Egg and Griddled Ham Breakfast Sandwiches
Total **30 min**; Makes **12**

- 1 dozen large eggs
  Kosher salt and pepper
- 6 oz. thinly sliced baked ham
- 1 cup chopped mixed herbs, such as parsley, tarragon and chives
- 1 Tbsp. fresh lemon juice
- 6 slider buns, split and lightly toasted

1. Preheat the oven to 350°. Pour 1 tablespoon of water into each cup of a 12-cup muffin pan. Crack an egg into each cup and season with salt and pepper. Bake the eggs for 13 to 15 minutes, until the whites are just firm and the yolks are still runny. Using a slotted spoon, immediately transfer the eggs to a plate.

2. Meanwhile, in a medium skillet, cook the ham over moderate heat, turning, until hot, about 2 minutes. In a small bowl, toss the herbs with the lemon juice and season with salt and pepper.

3. Arrange the split buns cut side up on a platter. Top with the ham, eggs and herbs. Serve open-face.

Chickpeas with Eggs and Mustard Greens

Total **30 min**; Serves **6**

- 6 **large eggs**
  Kosher salt and pepper
- ¼ **cup extra-virgin olive oil**
- 4 **shallots, thinly sliced**
- 6 **garlic cloves, thinly sliced**
- 1 **Fresno chile, seeded and thinly sliced**
  Two 15-oz. cans chickpeas, rinsed and drained
- 2½ **cups chicken stock or low-sodium broth**
- 4 **oz. mustard greens, stemmed, leaves torn**

1. Preheat the oven to 350°. Pour 1 tablespoon of water into 6 cups of a 12-cup muffin pan. Crack an egg into each of the 6 water-filled cups and season with salt and pepper. Bake the eggs for 13 to 15 minutes, until the whites are just firm and the yolks are still runny. Using a slotted spoon, immediately transfer the eggs to a plate.

2. Meanwhile, in a large skillet, heat the olive oil. Add the shallots, garlic and chile and cook over moderate heat until softened, about 5 minutes. Stir in the chickpeas and stock and bring to a boil. Add the mustard greens and cook until just wilted, about 3 minutes. Season with salt and pepper. Ladle into 6 bowls, top with the eggs and serve.

Warm Lentils with Smoked Trout and Poached Eggs

Total **30 min**; Serves **6**

- 1½ **cups green lentils**
- 8 **oz. boneless smoked trout fillet, skin removed, trout broken up into large flakes**
- 5 **oz. baby spinach**
- ⅓ **cup snipped chives**
- ¼ **cup fresh lemon juice**
- 3 **Tbsp. extra-virgin olive oil**
  Kosher salt and pepper
- 6 **large eggs**

1. Preheat the oven to 350°. In a medium saucepan, cover the lentils with water and bring to a boil. Simmer over moderate heat until tender, about 20 minutes. Drain well and transfer to a large bowl. Fold in the trout, spinach, chives, lemon juice and olive oil and season with salt and pepper.

2. Pour 1 tablespoon of water into 6 cups of a 12-cup muffin pan. Crack an egg into each of the 6 water-filled cups and season with salt and pepper. Bake the eggs for 13 to 15 minutes, until the whites are just firm and the yolks are still runny. Spoon the lentil salad onto plates. Using a slotted spoon, immediately transfer the eggs to the plates and serve.

BAKE HARD-SHELL TACOS

Fold tortillas in half and stuff them between the cups of an inverted muffin tin to form shells. Bake until crisp.

Chicken Tinga Tacos

Active **40 min**; Total **1 hr 30 min**; Serves **6**

- 2 **Tbsp. extra-virgin olive oil**
- 1 **white onion, thinly sliced**
- 4 **garlic cloves, sliced**
- 1½ **tsp. cumin seeds**
- 1½ **tsp. ground coriander**
- 2 **cups chicken stock or low-sodium broth**
- 14 **oz. tomato puree**
- 1 **oregano sprig**
- 2 **bay leaves**
- 4½ **lbs. skinless whole chicken legs**
- **Twelve 5-inch flour tortillas**
- 3 **Tbsp. distilled white vinegar**
- **Kosher salt and pepper**
- **Cilantro leaves, lime wedges and sliced onion, for serving**

1. In a large enameled cast-iron casserole, heat the olive oil. Add the onion, garlic, cumin and coriander and cook over moderate heat until the onion is softened, about 5 minutes. Add the stock, tomato puree, oregano and bay leaves and bring to a boil. Add the chicken, cover partially and simmer until cooked through, 35 to 40 minutes.

2. Meanwhile, preheat the oven to 400°. In batches, fold the tortillas in half and stuff them between the upturned cups of an inverted muffin tin to form shells. Bake for 15 minutes, until crisp.

3. Remove the chicken from the sauce and shred the meat. Return the meat to the sauce and simmer for 10 minutes. Discard the bay leaves and oregano sprig. Stir in the vinegar and season with salt and pepper. Serve the chicken tinga in the taco shells with cilantro, lime wedges and onion.

MAKE AHEAD The chicken tinga can be refrigerated for up to 2 days. Reheat gently before serving.

MAKE CRISPY TORTILLA BOWLS

I love ordering taco salads at restaurants, but I've never made them at home because the last thing I want to do is deep-fry. But now I can bake four tortilla bowls at once and they come out crunchy without all that oil.

 Invert a muffin tin. Gently stuff tortillas between upturned muffin cups to form bowls. Bake until crisp.

Shrimp Taco Salad Bowls

Total **45 min**; Serves **4**

   Four 10-inch flour tortillas

⅓   cup mayonnaise

2½ Tbsp. fresh lime juice

½   tsp. ground cumin

8   cups shredded green and red cabbage (1 lb.)

1   cup chopped cilantro, plus more for serving

3   pickled jalapeños, seeded and thinly sliced (¼ cup)

   Kosher salt and pepper

¾   lb. large shrimp, shelled and deveined

¾   tsp. chili powder

2   Tbsp. extra-virgin olive oil

   Sliced radishes and diced avocado, for serving

1. Preheat the oven to 400°. Invert 2 jumbo muffin tins on a work surface. Gently stuff the tortillas between the upturned muffin cups to form 4 bowls. Bake for 15 minutes, until crisp; let cool. (If you have only 1 jumbo muffin tin, do this in batches.)

2. Meanwhile, in a large bowl, whisk the mayonnaise, lime juice and cumin. Add the cabbage, 1 cup of cilantro and the jalapeños and toss. Season the slaw with salt and pepper.

3. In a medium bowl, toss the shrimp and chili powder; season with salt and pepper. In a large skillet, heat the olive oil until shimmering. Add the shrimp and cook over moderately high heat, turning once, until just white throughout, about 3 minutes. Transfer to a plate.

4. Fill the taco shells with the slaw and shrimp. Sprinkle with chopped cilantro, radishes and diced avocado. Serve.

MAKE AHEAD The taco shell bowls can be made up to 6 hours ahead.

VARIATION You can fill a bowl with guacamole. I like to call this "guacabowle."

BAKE APPLE PIE ROSES

Apple pie roses totally won the Internet. They were on Instagram, Pinterest...everywhere, because they're so pretty! I must have tested this excellent version almost 100 times to make sure that the puff pastry bakes all the way through.

STEP 1 Roll out a sheet of puff pastry and cut into 12 rectangles. Freeze until just chilled.

STEP 2 Spread apricot preserves on each pastry rectangle.

STEP 3 Arrange a layer of apple slices on the top half of the rectangle, overlapping them slightly.

STEP 4 Sprinkle the apple and pastry with cinnamon sugar.

STEP 5 Fold the pastry over the apple slices.

STEP 6 Loosely roll up the pastry and apples to form a rose.

STEP 7 Transfer each apple pie rose to a cup in a muffin pan and bake.

Apple Pie Roses

Active **40 min**; Total **1 hr 45 min**; Makes **12**

   All-purpose flour, for dusting

   One ½-lb. sheet of frozen puff pastry, thawed

2   **Tbsp. granulated sugar**

2   **tsp. cinnamon**

½   **tsp. kosher salt**

¼   **cup apricot preserves mixed with 1 Tbsp. hot water**

2   **Granny Smith apples—halved lengthwise, cored and very thinly sliced lengthwise to form half-moons**

   Confectioners' sugar, for dusting

1. Preheat the oven to 325°. On a lightly floured work surface, roll out the pastry to a 12-by-14-inch rectangle. Using a sharp knife, cut the pastry into twelve 2-by-7-inch rectangles. Transfer to a baking sheet and freeze until just chilled, about 5 minutes.

2. Lightly coat a 12-cup muffin tin with nonstick spray. In a small bowl, mix the granulated sugar with the cinnamon and salt. Work with one piece of pastry at a time, with a long side facing you: Spread 1 teaspoon of the apricot preserves on the pastry. Arrange a layer of apple slices on the top half of the rectangle, overlapping them slightly. Sprinkle the apple and pastry with the cinnamon sugar. Fold the pastry over the apples. Starting at a short side, loosely roll up the pastry and apples to form a rose; transfer to one of the prepared muffin cups. Repeat with the remaining pastry, preserves, apple slices and cinnamon sugar to form 11 more roses.

3. Bake the apple pie roses for about 50 minutes, until puffed and golden. Transfer to a rack to cool slightly. Dust the apple pie roses with confectioners' sugar and serve them warm or at room temperature.

MAKE AHEAD The apple pie roses can be stored in an airtight container overnight. Rewarm if desired.

OVEN

RIPEN BANANAS ASAP

Overripe bananas—supersweet and packed with flavor—are essential for banana bread. But I don't always plan ahead. So when I only have green bananas, I use this hack for ripening them: I bake them whole in the oven until they get soft, then spoon out the flesh.

 Bake underripe bananas in a 350° oven until the peels are dark all over and the fruit is soft to the touch, 5 to 7 minutes. Slice through the peels lengthwise to scoop out the fruit.

Chocolate Chunk Banana Bread

Active **30 min;** Total **1 hr 40 min plus cooling;** Makes **one 9-inch loaf**

- 1 **stick unsalted butter, melted and cooled slightly, plus more for greasing**
- 1½ **cups plus 1 Tbsp. all-purpose flour, plus more for dusting**
- ½ **cup walnuts**
- ½ **cup semisweet chocolate chunks or coarsely chopped chocolate (2½ oz.)**
- 1 **tsp. baking soda**
- ¾ **tsp. kosher salt**
- 1¼ **cups sugar, plus more for sprinkling**
- 1 **cup mashed very ripe banana**
- 2 **large eggs**

1. Preheat the oven to 350°. Coat a 9-by-5-inch metal loaf pan with butter and flour. Spread the walnuts in a pie plate and toast for about 7 minutes, until fragrant. Let cool, then coarsely chop. In a small bowl, toss the walnuts and chocolate chunks with 1 tablespoon of the flour.

2. In a medium bowl, whisk the remaining 1½ cups of flour with the baking soda and salt. In a large bowl, whisk the 1¼ cups of sugar with the banana, melted butter and eggs. Add the dry ingredients and whisk until smooth. Fold in the walnuts and chocolate chunks. Scrape the batter into the prepared pan and smooth the top. Sprinkle the top generously with sugar.

3. Bake the banana bread for about 1 hour, until a toothpick inserted in the center comes out clean. Let cool completely on a rack before turning out onto a platter. Cut into slices and serve.

MAKE AHEAD The banana bread can be stored in an airtight container for up to 5 days.

PEEL CHERRY TOMATOES

 Roast cherry tomatoes just until the skins wrinkle. Let them cool, then simply pinch off the skins.

Bucatini with Oven-Roasted Tomato Sauce

Total **30 min**; Serves **6**

1½ lbs. Campari tomatoes or large cherry tomatoes (not grape tomatoes)

1 small red onion, halved and very thinly sliced

2 Tbsp. capers—rinsed, drained and finely chopped

2 Tbsp. extra-virgin olive oil

3 garlic cloves, very thinly sliced

Kosher salt and pepper

1 lb. bucatini

Shaved or grated Parmigiano-Reggiano cheese, for serving

1. Preheat the oven to 500°. Line a large rimmed baking sheet with parchment paper. Spread the tomatoes on the baking sheet. Roast for 3 to 5 minutes, until the skins just wrinkle. Let cool slightly, then pull off and discard the skins.

2. On the baking sheet, toss the tomatoes with the onion, capers, olive oil, garlic and a generous pinch each of salt and pepper. Roast for about 5 minutes, until the tomatoes just start to burst and the onion is just softened.

3. Meanwhile, in a large saucepan of salted boiling water, cook the pasta until al dente. Drain well, reserving ½ cup of the cooking water.

4. Scrape the tomato sauce and any juices into the large saucepan. Add the pasta and cooking water and toss well. Season with salt and pepper and toss again. Transfer to shallow bowls, top with shaved or grated Parmesan and serve right away.

REVIVE STALE BREAD

Here's the problem: T minus 30 minutes until guests come for dinner and you find out that your baguette is stale. Here's a tip that will save the day. Wet the bread slightly, then pop it in the oven. It will emerge so crisp and crunchy, you'll be deafened by the noise when you bite into it. This trick also works beautifully for reviving any extra rustic bread or rolls you keep in the freezer.

 Run an unsliced stale or frozen loaf of bread under water to dampen it. Bake in a 350° oven until crisp on the outside and softened inside, 5 to 10 minutes.

Tuna Banh Mi

Total **20 min**; Serves **4**

New York City has a bunch of shops that specialize in banh mi. But there's one filling I've never seen in these Vietnamese sandwiches: canned tuna. So I made my own version with fresh mint leaves and sliced pickles for extra tang.

- **15 oz. tuna in olive oil, drained**
- **¼ cup fresh lime juice**
- **2 Tbsp. Asian fish sauce**
- **1 jalapeño, minced**

    Kosher salt and pepper

    One 24- to 32-inch soft baguette, split and toasted

    Mayonnaise, mint leaves, julienned carrots and sliced dill pickles, for serving

In a medium bowl, toss the tuna with the lime juice, fish sauce and jalapeño. Season with salt and pepper. Spread the cut sides of the baguette with mayonnaise, then fill with the tuna salad, mint, carrots and pickles. Close, cut into 4 sandwiches and serve.

Shrimp and Chorizo Tortas

Total **20 min**; Serves **4**

- **2 Tbsp. canola oil**
- **¾ lb. shelled and deveined medium shrimp**
- **½ lb. fresh chorizo, casing removed, meat crumbled**
- **¾ cup minced red onion**
- **1 garlic clove, minced**
- **2 Tbsp. fresh lime juice**

    Kosher salt and pepper

    Toasted kaiser rolls, mayonnaise, lettuce and thinly sliced tomato and avocado, for serving

In a large skillet, heat the canola oil. Add the shrimp, chorizo, onion and garlic and cook over high heat, stirring occasionally, until browned and the shrimp and chorizo are cooked through, about 8 minutes. Stir in the lime juice and 2 tablespoons of water and season with salt and pepper. Serve on toasted kaiser rolls with mayonnaise, lettuce, tomato and avocado.

BAKE DRIED PASTA

This tip for making pasta without boiling it in a pot of water is going to change your life. Combining uncooked pasta with sauce and water in a baking dish not only saves you time and dirties one less pot, it results in a surprisingly luscious dish.

Layer dried pasta with meatballs, cheese and sauce in a baking dish. Add water, cover tightly with foil, then bake.

Baked Ziti with Meatballs

Active **30 min**; Total **1 hr 45 min**
Serves **6 to 8**

- ½ **lb. ground pork**
- ½ **lb. ground beef**
- ½ **cup plain dry bread crumbs**
- 2 **large eggs, lightly beaten**
- ⅓ **cup lightly packed torn basil, plus more for garnish**
- ¼ **cup freshly grated Parmigiano-Reggiano cheese, plus more for serving**
- **Kosher salt and pepper**
- 1 **lb. ziti or rigatoni**
- 1 **lb. fresh mozzarella, torn into 1-inch pieces**
- 3 **cups marinara sauce**

1. Preheat the oven to 400°. In a large bowl, combine the pork, beef, bread crumbs, eggs, ⅓ cup of torn basil, ¼ cup of Parmesan and 1 teaspoon each of salt and pepper; mix well. Form the mixture into 1-inch balls.

2. In a 9-by-13-inch ceramic baking dish, spread half of the pasta in an even layer. Arrange half of the meatballs and mozzarella on the pasta. Spoon half of the marinara on top and season with ½ teaspoon of salt. Repeat with the remaining pasta, meatballs, mozzarella and marinara, then season with ½ teaspoon of salt. Add 2½ cups of water to the baking dish and cover tightly with foil.

3. Bake for about 1 hour, until the pasta is tender and most of the liquid is absorbed. Uncover and bake for 5 minutes longer, then turn on the broiler and broil 8 inches from the heat until the top is lightly browned. Let stand for 5 minutes, then garnish the baked ziti with basil and Parmesan and serve.

MAKE AHEAD The baked pasta can be refrigerated overnight. Reheat gently.

VARIATION You can use other pasta shapes in place of the ziti or rigatoni. Try curly rotini or fusilli, shells or campanelle, which look like little bells.

PLASTIC BAGGIE

MAKE PANCAKES

STEP 1 Set a large resealable plastic bag in a tall bowl or measuring cup to hold it upright. Mix pancake batter inside the bag.

STEP 2 Gently twist the bag and snip off a bottom corner.

STEP 3 Pipe 4-inch rounds of batter onto the griddle.

Rye Pancakes with Maple Caramelized Pears

📷 PAGE 174

Total **40 min**; Serves **4**

- 5 **Tbsp. melted unsalted butter, plus more for brushing**
- 2 **Bartlett pears—peeled, cored and cut into ¾-inch pieces**
- ¾ **cup pure maple syrup**
    Kosher salt
- 2 **cups whole milk**
- 2 **large eggs**
- 1 **cup rye flour**
- ¾ **cup all-purpose flour**
- 3 **Tbsp. sugar**
- 2 **tsp. baking powder**

1. In a large skillet, heat 2 tablespoons of the butter. Add the pears and cook over moderately high heat, stirring occasionally, until just tender and golden, about 5 minutes. Stir in the maple syrup, season with salt and keep warm.

2. Set a large resealable plastic bag in a tall bowl to hold it upright. In the bag, whisk the milk with the eggs and the remaining 3 tablespoons of melted butter, then add both flours, the sugar, baking powder and ¾ teaspoon of salt; stir until incorporated.

3. Heat a griddle and brush lightly with melted butter. Gently twist the bag and hold it upright. Using scissors, snip off ¼ inch from a bottom corner. For each batch of pancakes, pipe 4-inch rounds of batter onto the griddle. Cook over moderate heat until bubbles appear on the surface of the pancakes, 2 to 3 minutes. Flip and cook until risen and golden brown, 2 minutes longer. Serve topped with the maple pears.

CONTINUED ▶

Whole-Wheat Pancakes with Roasted Berries

Total **35 min**; Serves **4**

- 3 cups mixed berries, such as blueberries, raspberries and halved strawberries
- ¼ cup plus 3 Tbsp. granulated sugar
- 1½ cups whole milk
- 2 large eggs
- 3 Tbsp. melted unsalted butter, plus more for brushing
- 1 cup all-purpose flour
- ¾ cup whole-wheat flour
- 2 tsp. baking powder
- ¾ tsp. kosher salt
- Whipped cream and confectioners' sugar, for topping

1. Preheat the oven to 350°. On a rimmed baking sheet, toss the berries with ¼ cup of the granulated sugar. Bake for about 10 minutes, until the berries are just softened.

2. Meanwhile, set a large resealable plastic bag in a tall bowl to hold it upright. In the bag, whisk the milk with the eggs and the 3 tablespoons of melted butter, then add both flours, the remaining 3 tablespoons of granulated sugar, the baking powder and salt; stir until incorporated.

3. Heat a griddle and brush lightly with melted butter. Gently twist the bag and hold it upright; snip off ¼ inch from a bottom corner. For each batch, pipe 4-inch rounds of batter onto the griddle. Cook over moderate heat until bubbles appear on the surface of the pancakes, 2 to 3 minutes. Flip and cook until risen and golden brown, 2 minutes longer. Transfer to plates and top with the berries, whipped cream and confectioners' sugar.

FORM GNOCCHI

You can make the easiest gnocchi in history with this trick. There's no rolling involved. Just cut the dough into perfect little dumplings.

 STEP 1 Tie a length of thin kitchen twine tightly across the handles of a saucepan.

STEP 2 Add gnocchi dough to a resealable plastic bag; press the dough into a corner of the bag to remove as much air as possible, then snip off the corner.

STEP 3 Pipe out gnocchi dough into boiling water, using the twine to cut each dumpling.

Ricotta Gnocchi with Summer Herbs

Total **45 min**; Serves **4 to 6**

Kosher salt and pepper

2 cups fresh ricotta cheese

1 large egg

¼ cup freshly grated Parmigiano-Reggiano cheese

¾ cup all-purpose flour

2 Tbsp. extra-virgin olive oil, plus more for greasing and drizzling

1½ tsp. finely grated lemon zest, plus more for sprinkling

Snipped chives, chopped parsley and small basil leaves, for garnish

1. Tie thin kitchen twine tightly across a large, two-handled saucepan. Fill the saucepan with water and bring to a simmer. Add a generous pinch of salt.

2. Meanwhile, in a food processor, pulse the ricotta with the egg and cheese until smooth; scrape down the side of the bowl as necessary. Add the flour and 1½ teaspoons of salt and pulse until just incorporated.

3. Scrape the gnocchi dough into a large sturdy resealable plastic bag; press the dough into a corner of the bag to remove as much air as possible, then snip off the corner to make a ½- to ¾-inch opening.

4. Using steady pressure and working over the pot of simmering water, pipe out one-third of the gnocchi dough into ¾-inch pieces, using the twine to cut them into the saucepan. Simmer until the gnocchi rise to the surface, then continue simmering until they're plumped and just cooked through, about 5 minutes total. Using a slotted spoon, transfer the gnocchi to a lightly oiled rimmed baking sheet. Repeat with the remaining dough in 2 batches.

5. Transfer the gnocchi to a platter. Add the 2 tablespoons of olive oil and the 1½ teaspoons of lemon zest and gently toss to coat. Season with salt and pepper and toss again. Serve in shallow bowls, garnished with a drizzle of olive oil, grated lemon zest, snipped chives, chopped parsley and small basil leaves.

MAKE AHEAD The cooked gnocchi can be refrigerated overnight. Reheat in simmering water for 1 minute before serving.

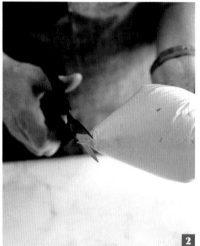

POUND GARLIC PASTE

This plastic baggie hack is a lifesaver for smashing a lot of garlic at once. Bonus: My hands and cutting board don't reek afterward!

STEP 1 Place peeled garlic cloves in a small resealable plastic bag. Add a pinch of salt.

STEP 2 Using a rolling pin or meat mallet, gently crush the garlic. Continue to crush the garlic, scraping it to the bottom of the bag occasionally, until a paste forms.

STEP 3 Refrigerate the paste in the bag or cut off a corner and squeeze the paste into a bowl.

Garlic Oil–Basted Shrimp Skewers

Total **35 min**; Serves **4**

- 3 garlic cloves
- Kosher salt and black pepper
- ¼ cup extra-virgin olive oil, plus more for greasing
- 2 tsp. finely chopped thyme
- 1 tsp. finely grated lemon zest
- ¼ tsp. crushed red pepper
- 20 shelled and deveined large shrimp
- 2 medium yellow squash, shaved lengthwise with a wide vegetable peeler
- 4 long wooden skewers, soaked in water for 30 minutes
- Lemon wedges, for serving

1. Put the garlic in a small resealable plastic bag. Add a generous pinch of salt and, using a rolling pin or meat mallet, gently crush the garlic until juices start to form. Continue to crush the garlic, scraping it to the bottom of the bag occasionally, until a paste forms. Cut off a corner of the bag and squeeze the paste into a small bowl, then whisk in the ¼ cup of olive oil, the thyme, lemon zest and crushed red pepper.

2. Light a grill or heat a grill pan and oil the grate. Alternately thread the shrimp and squash ribbons onto the skewers and season with salt and pepper. Grill the skewers over high heat, basting with the garlic oil and turning once, until the shrimp are white throughout and the squash are lightly charred, about 5 minutes. Serve with lemon wedges.

CONTINUED ▶

▶ CONTINUED

POUND
GARLIC
PASTE

Spicy Garlic Bread Bites

Total **25 min;** Serves **4**

Serve these as hors d'oeuvres, in a salad or at the table.

- **3 garlic cloves**
- **Kosher salt and pepper**
- **1 to 2 chiles de árbol, crushed**
- **4 Tbsp. unsalted butter, melted**
- **½ lb. sourdough bread, torn into 2-inch pieces**
- **2 Tbsp. finely chopped parsley**

1. Preheat the oven to 400°. Put the garlic in a small resealable plastic bag. Add a generous pinch of salt and, using a rolling pin or meat mallet, gently crush the garlic until juices start to form. Continue to crush the garlic, scraping it to the bottom of the bag occasionally, until a paste forms.

2. Cut off a corner of the bag and scrape the garlic paste into a large bowl; whisk in the crushed chile de árbol and melted butter. Add the bread, season generously with salt and pepper and toss well.

3. Spread the bread on a large rimmed baking sheet. Bake for 12 to 15 minutes, until crisp on the outside but chewy in the middle. Transfer to a serving bowl, garnish with the chopped parsley and serve warm.

POACH SALMON

If you love ordering poached salmon at restaurants, I have a plastic bag hack that lets you re-create that yummy dish at home. You can cook perfectly medium-rare (or medium, or medium-well) salmon by poaching fillets in resealable BPA-free plastic baggies. My apologies to seafood restaurants everywhere, which are about to lose money on this one.

 Lay a salmon (or other fish) fillet in a resealable BPA-free plastic bag—look for the wording on the box. Seal and poach in simmering water.

Poached Salmon Salad with Bibb and Peas

Active **35 min**; Total **50 min**; Serves **4**

SALMON

    One 1-lb. skinless salmon fillet

    Kosher salt and pepper

½ lemon, thinly sliced

2 tarragon sprigs

SALAD

    Kosher salt and pepper

6 oz. snap peas, strings removed

1 cup frozen peas, thawed

3 Tbsp. Champagne vinegar

1½ Tbsp. minced shallot

1 Tbsp. Dijon mustard

¼ cup extra-virgin olive oil

1½ Tbsp. finely chopped tarragon plus ¼ cup leaves

1 large head of Bibb lettuce, cored and leaves torn

1. Make the salmon Bring a large, deep skillet of water to a simmer. Season the salmon fillet with salt and pepper and place in a large resealable BPA-free plastic bag. Set the lemon slices and tarragon sprigs on the fillet and seal the bag, pressing out the air. Put the bag in the skillet and poach the salmon at a gentle simmer until just cooked through, about 10 minutes. Transfer to a plate and let cool slightly, then open the bag and slide the salmon onto the plate. Let cool completely, then flake into 2-inch pieces.

2. Make the salad Empty the skillet and fill it with water. Bring the water to a boil and season generously with salt. Add both peas and cook until crisp-tender, 1 to 2 minutes. Drain well and cool under running water, then drain on paper towels.

3. In a large serving bowl, whisk the vinegar with the shallot and mustard, then gradually whisk in the oil until combined. Stir in the finely chopped tarragon and season with salt and pepper. Add the lettuce, both peas and the tarragon leaves and toss well. Season with salt and pepper and toss again. Add the salmon and very gently fold to mix. Serve right away.

MAKE AHEAD The poached salmon can be refrigerated overnight. Let stand at room temperature for 15 minutes before assembling the salad.

PIPE FROZEN YOGURT DOTS

A shout-out to my friend and *Top Chef* judge Gail Simmons, who shared this trick for frozen yogurt dots. They're super-simple, fast and healthy.

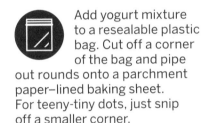 Add yogurt mixture to a resealable plastic bag. Cut off a corner of the bag and pipe out rounds onto a parchment paper–lined baking sheet. For teeny-tiny dots, just snip off a smaller corner.

Frozen Yogurt Drops with Strawberries and Pistachios

Total **15 min plus 3 hr freezing**
Makes **2 dozen**

½ **cup fat-free Greek yogurt**

2 **Tbsp. honey**

Pinch of kosher salt

Finely chopped strawberries and pistachios, for sprinkling

In a small bowl, whisk the yogurt, honey and salt. Scrape the mixture into a resealable plastic sandwich bag; snip off about ⅛ inch from a bottom corner of the bag. Pipe 1-inch rounds onto a parchment paper–lined baking sheet. Sprinkle each drop with chopped strawberries and pistachios. Freeze until very firm, about 3 hours. Serve frozen.

SWIRL FROSTING

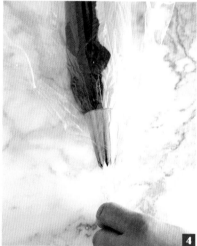

Why choose between chocolate and vanilla frosting when you can have both? The contrast of black and white twists makes the cupcakes look even yummier.

 STEP 1 Lay a large sheet of plastic wrap on a work surface with a long side facing you. Using a small spatula, spread the vanilla frosting in a 3-inch-wide strip down the center of the plastic. Spread the chocolate frosting in a 3-inch-wide strip alongside the vanilla.

STEP 2 Using the plastic, fold the vanilla frosting over the chocolate, twisting one end of the plastic to seal and form a pouch.

STEPS 3 AND 4 Snip off a corner of a pastry bag or resealable plastic bag and fit the bag with a medium star tip. Pull the twisted end of the pouch through the star tip and cut off the protruding plastic. Refrigerate the frosting until barely firm, about 15 minutes.

STEP 5 Pipe the frosting onto the cupcakes and serve.

Black-and-White Cupcakes

Active **40 min**; Total **1 hr 30 min**
Makes **12**

CUPCAKES

- 1 **cup all-purpose flour**
- ⅓ **cup unsweetened cocoa powder**
- ½ **tsp. baking powder**
- ½ **tsp. kosher salt**
- ¼ **tsp. baking soda**
- 6 **Tbsp. unsalted butter, softened**
- ¾ **cup granulated sugar**
- 2 **large eggs**
- ½ **cup sour cream**
- 2½ **tsp. pure vanilla extract**

FROSTING

- 2 **sticks unsalted butter, softened**
- 4 **cups confectioners' sugar**
- 2 **tsp. pure vanilla extract**
- ½ **tsp. kosher salt**
- ¼ **cup milk**
- ½ **cup unsweetened cocoa powder**

1. Make the cupcakes Preheat the oven to 350° and line a 12-cup muffin pan with paper liners. In a medium bowl, whisk the flour with the cocoa powder, baking powder, salt and baking soda. In a large bowl, using a hand mixer, beat the butter with the granulated sugar at medium-high speed until fluffy. Beat in the eggs one at a time, then beat in the sour cream and vanilla until smooth. At low speed, beat in the dry ingredients. Scoop the batter into the lined muffin cups.

2. Bake the cupcakes in the center of the oven for about 17 minutes, until springy and a toothpick inserted in the centers comes out clean. Let cool slightly in the pan, then transfer the cupcakes to a rack to cool completely.

3. Meanwhile, make the frosting In a large bowl, using a hand mixer, beat the butter at medium speed until smooth. Add the confectioners' sugar, vanilla, salt and 2 tablespoons of the milk and beat at low speed just until combined, then beat at medium speed until smooth. Scrape half of the vanilla frosting into a medium bowl. Add the cocoa powder and the remaining 2 tablespoons of milk to the frosting in the large bowl and beat at low speed until fully incorporated.

4. Frost the cupcakes following the steps on the opposite page.

ICE CREAM SHORTCUT

Make ice cream without the machine with my cheater's method.

STEP 1 Pour the ice cream base (custard) into a resealable plastic bag. Freeze the bag flat.

STEP 2 Pulse the frozen custard in a food processor until smooth.

STEP 3 Transfer the ice cream to a loaf pan. Fold in toppings and freeze until firm.

Vanilla-Almond Ice Cream with Cherries and Pistachios

Active **45 min**; Total **8 hr 45 min plus 6 hr freezing**; Makes **about 1 qt.**

- 6 large egg yolks
- 1½ cups heavy cream
- 1½ cups whole milk
- ¾ cup sugar
- ¾ tsp. kosher salt
- 1 vanilla bean, split lengthwise and seeds scraped
- ½ tsp. pure almond extract
- ¾ cup fresh cherries, pitted and halved
- ¼ cup shelled pistachios, coarsely chopped

1. Set a medium bowl in a large bowl of ice water. In another medium bowl, beat the egg yolks until pale, 1 to 2 minutes.

2. In a medium saucepan, whisk the cream with the milk, sugar, salt and the vanilla bean and seeds. Bring to a simmer, whisking, until the sugar is completely dissolved. Very gradually whisk half of the hot cream mixture into the beaten egg yolks in a thin stream, then whisk this mixture into the saucepan.

Cook over moderately low heat, stirring constantly with a wooden spoon, until the custard is thick enough to lightly coat the back of the spoon, about 12 minutes; don't let it boil.

3. Strain the custard through a medium-mesh strainer into the bowl set in the ice water; discard the vanilla bean. Let the custard cool completely, stirring occasionally. Stir in the almond extract. Pour into a large resealable freezer bag and seal, pressing out the air. Lay the bag flat in the freezer and freeze until firm, at least 8 hours or overnight.

4. Working quickly, in batches if necessary, transfer the frozen custard to the bowl of a food processor. Pulse at 5-second intervals until smooth. Transfer the custard to a chilled 9-by-4-inch metal loaf pan and fold in the cherries and pistachios. Cover with plastic wrap and freeze until firm, about 6 hours or overnight.

MAKE AHEAD The ice cream can be frozen for up to 1 week.

VARIATION Instead of cherries and pistachios, fold in 1 cup of chopped chocolate-covered pretzels or chopped halvah.

PLASTIC LIDS

SLICE CHERRY TOMATOES

Instead of halving cherry tomatoes one at a time, here's a superfast way to slice a bunch at once.

 STEP 1 Place cherry tomatoes between two plastic takeout container lids.

STEP 2 Pressing down gently, cut the tomatoes in half with a sharp knife. You could use a serrated knife, but I prefer a chef's knife.

STEP 3 Transfer your halved cherry tomatoes to a bowl.

Cherry Tomato and Piquillo Pepper Fattoush
Total **45 min**; Serves **4 to 6**

- 3 **pita breads, split and halved**
- ¼ **cup extra-virgin olive oil, plus more for brushing**
- **Ground sumac, for seasoning**
- **Kosher salt and pepper**
- 3 **Tbsp. red wine vinegar**
- 1 **Tbsp. Dijon mustard**
- **Two 6- to 8-oz. romaine hearts, torn into bite-size pieces**
- 8 **jarred piquillo peppers, cut into bite-size pieces (¾ cup)**
- 8 **radishes, thinly sliced**
- 1 **pint cherry tomatoes, halved**
- 3 **Persian cucumbers, thinly sliced**
- 1 **cup mint leaves**
- ¾ **cup snipped chives**
- ½ **cup snipped dill**

1. Preheat the oven to 400°. Arrange the pita on a large baking sheet. Brush with olive oil and season with sumac, salt and pepper. Bake for 12 to 15 minutes, until golden and crisp. Let cool, then break into bite-size pieces.

2. Meanwhile, in a large serving bowl, whisk the vinegar with the mustard and ¼ cup of olive oil until incorporated. Season with salt and pepper. Add the romaine, peppers, radishes, tomatoes, cucumbers, mint, chives and dill; toss well. Add the pita chips, season with salt and pepper and toss again. Sprinkle with sumac and serve.

MAKE AHEAD The pita chips can be stored in an airtight container for up to 2 days.

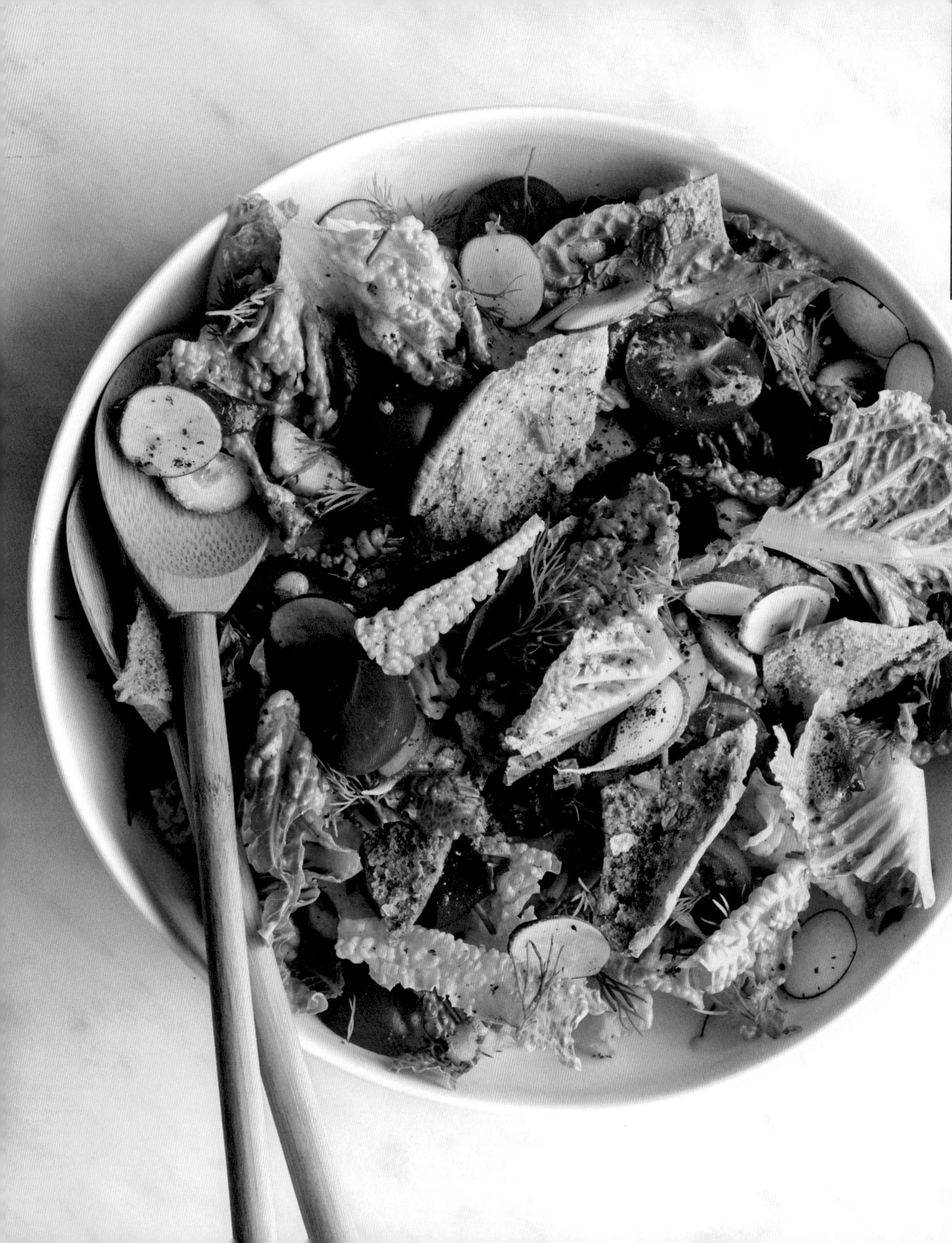

PIT OLIVES

Let's say you have a lot of olives to pit but don't own an olive pitter. I have a simple solution: two plastic takeout lids. You'll get the job done quickly in batches. This method is practically mess-free to boot—no pits or olive meat smushed all over your work surface.

 Put olives on top of a plastic takeout lid and cover with another lid. Using your palm or a meat mallet, lightly crush the olives. Discard the pits. This trick works great with meaty olives like kalamatas or Castelvetranos.

Antipasto Salad Crostini

Total **30 min;** Makes **14**

When I have an antipasto platter at an Italian restaurant, I wrap the vegetables and cheese in slices of salami in order to get the perfect bite. That gave me the idea to chop up typical antipasto ingredients (olives, mozzarella cheese, salami) to mound on crostini.

½ cup Castelvetrano olives

½ cup finely diced mozzarella or pecorino cheese (2 oz.)

2 oz. sliced Genoa salami, finely chopped

1½ Tbsp. red wine vinegar

⅓ cup finely chopped parsley

½ tsp. crushed red pepper

¼ tsp. dried oregano

2½ Tbsp. extra-virgin olive oil, plus more for brushing

Kosher salt and black pepper

Fourteen ½-inch-thick diagonal slices of baguette

1 garlic clove

1. In batches, put the olives on the top of a plastic takeout lid and invert another lid on top. Using your palm or a meat mallet, lightly crush the olives. Discard the pits and finely chop the olives.

2. In a large bowl, toss the olives with the cheese, salami, vinegar, parsley, crushed red pepper, oregano and the 2½ tablespoons of olive oil. Season with salt and black pepper.

3. Light a grill or heat a grill pan. Brush the baguette slices with olive oil. Grill over moderately high heat, turning once, until lightly charred, 2 to 3 minutes. Transfer to a platter and rub with the garlic clove. Spoon the antipasto salad on top of the crostini and serve.

MAKE AHEAD The antipasto salad can be refrigerated overnight.

SHAPE BURGER PATTIES

To form patties that cook evenly and look stellar on big brioche buns, I mound 6 ounces of ground meat on a plastic takeout lid, invert another lid on top, then press down to flatten.

CONTINUED ▶

▶ CONTINUED

SHAPE
BURGER
PATTIES

Green Goddess Turkey Burgers

Total **30 min**; Serves **4**

I love green goddess dip for vegetables. Inspired by those flavors, I mixed anchovy, scallions and lots of fresh herbs into my turkey burgers.

1½ lbs. ground turkey

⅓ cup finely chopped basil

⅓ cup finely chopped scallions

⅓ cup finely chopped parsley

1 Tbsp. minced anchovy

   Kosher salt and pepper

⅓ cup mayonnaise, plus more for serving

4 large hamburger buns, such as brioche, split and toasted

   Sliced red onion and baby greens, for serving

1. In a large bowl, using a fork, gently stir the turkey with the basil, scallions, parsley, anchovy, 1 teaspoon of salt, ½ teaspoon of pepper and the ⅓ cup of mayonnaise. Using two 4-inch round plastic takeout lids, press the turkey mixture into 4 patties. Transfer to a plate.

2. Light a grill or heat a grill pan. Season the patties lightly with salt and pepper and grill over moderately high heat, turning once, until cooked through, about 8 minutes. Transfer the burgers to the buns, top with mayonnaise, onion and greens and serve.

MAKE AHEAD The patties can be refrigerated for up to 3 hours before grilling.

Bloody Mary Burgers

Total **30 min**; Serves **4**

I season these juicy beef burgers with zippy ingredients you'd typically find in a Bloody Mary.

1½ lbs. ground sirloin

3 Tbsp. prepared horseradish, drained

3 Tbsp. tomato paste

2 tsp. hot sauce

2 tsp. Worcestershire sauce

1½ tsp. celery seeds

   Kosher salt and pepper

4 large hamburger buns, such as brioche, split and toasted

   Mayonnaise, red leaf lettuce, sliced tomato and American cheese, for serving

1. In a medium bowl, using a fork, gently stir the ground sirloin with the horseradish, tomato paste, hot sauce, Worcestershire, celery seeds and 1 teaspoon each of salt and pepper. Using two 4-inch round plastic takeout lids, press the beef mixture into 4 patties. Transfer to a plate.

2. Light a grill or heat a grill pan. Season the patties lightly with salt and pepper and grill over moderate heat, turning once, until medium-rare within, 8 to 10 minutes. Transfer the burgers to the buns, top with mayonnaise, lettuce, tomato and cheese and serve.

MAKE AHEAD The patties can be refrigerated for up to 3 hours before grilling.

Cheater Chorizo Burgers

Total **30 min**; Serves **4**

To mimic the spicy, vibrant flavor of chorizo, I add chili powder, hot paprika, cumin and garlic to these pork burgers.

1½ lbs. ground pork

2½ Tbsp. distilled white vinegar

1 Tbsp. hot paprika

2 garlic cloves, minced

2 tsp. chili powder

1 tsp. ground cumin

1 tsp. dried oregano

   Kosher salt and pepper

4 large hamburger buns, such as brioche, split and toasted

   Ketchup, Bibb lettuce and sliced yellow tomato, for serving

1. In a medium bowl, using a fork, gently stir the pork with the vinegar, paprika, garlic, chili powder, cumin, oregano, 1 teaspoon of salt and ¾ teaspoon of pepper. Using two 4-inch round plastic takeout lids, press the pork mixture into 4 patties. Transfer to a plate.

2. Light a grill or heat a grill pan. Season the patties lightly with salt and pepper and grill over moderately high heat, turning once, until cooked through, about 8 minutes. Transfer the burgers to the buns, top with ketchup, lettuce and tomato and serve.

MAKE AHEAD The patties can be refrigerated for up to 3 hours before grilling.

CUT OUT LARGE COOKIES

I was planning to make sugar cookies at a friend's house when I realized she didn't have cookie cutters. That's when I got the idea to use a plastic takeout lid. I immediately loved the dramatic proportions of these giant cookies! They're fun to make for bake sales or to give as holiday gifts.

 Cut out large cookies with a paring knife using a plastic takeout lid as a template. You can also use the lid to cut out pie dough or puff pastry, as in the Kiwi Tartlets (p. 106).

Giant Sesame Cookies

Active **45 min;** Total **2 hr 15 min plus cooling;** Makes **8**

1½ cups all-purpose flour, plus more for dusting

½ tsp. baking powder

½ tsp. kosher salt

6 Tbsp. unsalted butter, softened

¾ cup sugar

1 large egg

1 tsp. pure vanilla extract

½ tsp. finely grated lemon zest

3 Tbsp. honey

1 Tbsp. hot water

Toasted white and black sesame seeds, for sprinkling

1. In a medium bowl, whisk the 1½ cups of flour with the baking powder and salt. In a large bowl, using a hand mixer, beat the butter with the sugar at medium-high speed until fluffy, about 2 minutes. Beat in the egg, vanilla and lemon zest. Add the dry ingredients and beat at medium speed until the dough comes together. Pat the cookie dough into two ½-inch-thick disks, wrap in plastic and refrigerate until chilled, about 45 minutes.

2. Preheat the oven to 350°. On a lightly floured surface, roll out the dough a scant ¼ inch thick. Using a 4-inch round plastic takeout lid, cut out the cookies as close together as possible. Reroll the scraps and cut out more cookies. Transfer the cookies to a large parchment paper–lined baking sheet and refrigerate until chilled, about 30 minutes.

3. Bake the cookies until lightly browned around the edges, about 15 minutes. Let the cookies cool on the baking sheet for 5 minutes, then transfer them to racks and let cool completely.

4. In a small bowl, whisk the honey with the hot water until dissolved. Lightly brush the cookies with the honey mixture and sprinkle with white and black sesame seeds. Let stand until dry before serving.

MAKE AHEAD The cookies can be stored in an airtight container for up to 3 days.

VARIATION For lemon–poppy seed cookies, in place of Step 4, whisk ½ cup of confectioners' sugar with 1½ tablespoons of milk, 1 tablespoon of fresh lemon juice and 1 teaspoon of poppy seeds. Brush the cooled cookies with the poppy seed glaze and let stand until set.

SCISSORS

BUTCHER CHICKEN

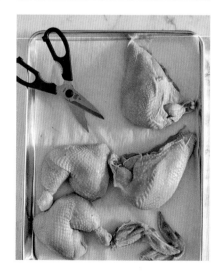

Cutting up a whole chicken can be a challenge. You don't know where the blade is going and you end up hacking the bird into awkward pieces. Scissors make it much easier to cut through cartilage. Just be sure to use sturdy poultry shears.

STEP 1 Set the chicken breast side down on a work surface. Cut off the wingettes and wing tips.

STEP 2 Cut along either side of the backbone to remove it.

STEP 3 Turn the chicken breast side up. Cut between one thigh and one side of the breast (where the skin is loose) to remove the leg. Repeat to remove the other leg.

STEP 4 Set the chicken breast side down on the work surface and flatten to expose the center breast bone, then remove it with your hands. Cut between the breast halves to split them.

Oven-BBQ Chicken

Active **45 min**; Total **1 hr 30 min**; Serves **6**

1½ cups ketchup

¼ cup plus 2 Tbsp. light brown sugar

¼ cup plus 2 Tbsp. gochujang
(Korean red pepper paste)

4½ Tbsp. distilled white vinegar

2 garlic cloves, finely grated

Two 3½-lb. whole chickens,
wingettes and wing tips removed,
chickens cut into 4 pieces each

Extra-virgin olive oil, for brushing

Kosher salt and pepper

Lime wedges, for serving

1. In a medium saucepan, whisk the ketchup, sugar, gochujang, vinegar and garlic. Bring to a boil over moderately high heat, then simmer over moderately low heat, stirring frequently, until slightly thickened, about 5 minutes. Let cool. Transfer ½ cup of the sauce to a small bowl and reserve for serving.

2. Meanwhile, preheat the oven to 425°. Line 2 large rimmed baking sheets with heavy-duty foil. Arrange the chicken parts on the prepared baking sheets, brush them all over with olive oil and season with salt and pepper.

3. Roast the chicken in the upper and lower thirds of the oven for 15 to 20 minutes, until the skin is very lightly browned. Brush the chicken with some of the sauce and roast for 10 minutes, until glazed. Flip the chicken and brush with sauce. Roast for 25 to 30 minutes longer, turning and brushing every 8 minutes, until the chicken is nicely glazed and an instant-read thermometer inserted in each piece registers 165°. Transfer to a platter and serve with lime wedges and the reserved sauce.

MAKE AHEAD The BBQ sauce can be refrigerated for up to 1 week.

SNIP HERBS

You could chop herbs with a knife, but why dirty up a cutting board if you don't have to? It's so much easier to grab a handful of herbs and cut them with kitchen shears right into your bowl.

 Snip fresh herbs with a pair of scissors until you reach the thick stems.

Herb and Bulgur Salad with Sunflower Seeds

Total **35 min;** Serves **6**

- 1 **cup medium bulgur**
- 2 **cups boiling water**
  Kosher salt and pepper
  One 2-oz. bunch of parsley
  One 2-oz. bunch of cilantro
  One 1-oz. bunch of chives
  One 1-oz. bunch of dill
- ½ **cup salted toasted sunflower seeds**
- ¼ **cup fresh lemon juice**
- 3 **Tbsp. extra-virgin olive oil**

1. In a large heatproof bowl, cover the bulgur with the boiling water. Add a generous pinch of salt, cover with plastic and let stand until the bulgur is tender and the water is absorbed, about 20 minutes. Fluff with a fork.

2. Hold the herb bunches together in one hand. Using scissors, snip the herbs over the bulgur until you reach the thick stems (you should have about 1½ cups each of parsley and cilantro and ¾ cup each of chives and dill); discard the stems. Add the sunflower seeds, lemon juice and olive oil to the bulgur and toss well. Season with salt and pepper and toss again. Serve at room temperature.

MAKE AHEAD The bulgur salad can be made early in the day. The cooked bulgur can be refrigerated for up to 3 days.

TRIM GREEN BEANS

Pinching off the woody stems of green beans one by one takes forever. It's so much easier to use a pair of kitchen scissors to slice off a bunch at a time.

Hold green beans with the woody stem ends all facing in one direction. Snip off the ends with scissors.

Charred Green Beans with Apricots

Total **20 min**; Serves **4**

I add sweet apricots to these fiery and fresh-tasting sautéed green beans.

1½ **Tbsp. canola oil**

½ **lb. haricots verts, trimmed**

3 **apricots—halved, pitted and cut into ¼-inch-thick wedges**

2 **Tbsp. fresh lime juice**

1 **Tbsp. Asian fish sauce**

1 **Thai chile, thinly sliced**

1 **cup mint leaves, chopped**

Kosher salt

In a large skillet, heat the oil until shimmering. Add the green beans and cook over high heat until charred on the bottom, about 4 minutes. Remove from the heat and stir in the apricots, lime juice, fish sauce, chile and mint. Season with salt. Transfer to a platter and serve.

more foods to scissor

PIZZA You may think it's crazy to cut pizza with scissors, but this is how lots of places in Italy do it, so you know it's legit. It's also less messy than cutting with a knife.

MEAT If you've ever gone to a Korean barbecue restaurant, you'll know this is how the servers cut up bite-size portions of grilled beef and pork. You could also use scissors to slice up ham and other cold cuts for salads.

CANNED TOMATOES If I need to chop canned whole tomatoes, I never pull out my cutting board. I just stick a pair of kitchen shears directly into the can and scissor away.

LINE A CAKE PAN

 STEP 1 Fold a 12-inch square of parchment paper in half to form a rectangle. Fold it in half again to form a square. With the folded edges on the left and bottom, bring the bottom right corner up to meet the left edge, making a triangle; fold the same way again.

STEP 2 Hold the sharpest point of the triangle in the center of an inverted round cake pan. Using scissors, cut the paper where it lines up with the edge of the pan.

STEP 3 Unfold the parchment and line your cake pan perfectly. For a video, go to: foodandwine.com/video/mad-genius-cooking-tips.

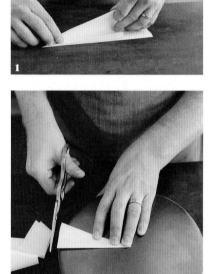

Espresso Snack Cake

Active **40 min;** Total **2 hr 15 min**
Makes **one 9-inch cake**

CAKE

- **4 Tbsp. unsalted butter,** melted and cooled slightly, plus more for greasing
- **1 cup all-purpose flour**
- **⅓ cup unsweetened cocoa powder**
- **1½ Tbsp. instant espresso powder**
- **1 tsp. baking soda**
- **¾ tsp. kosher salt**
- **1 large egg**
- **1 cup sugar**
- **½ cup buttermilk**
- **½ cup whole milk**
- **1 tsp. pure vanilla extract**

GANACHE

- **⅓ cup heavy cream**
- **1 Tbsp. sugar**
- **2 tsp. instant espresso powder**
- **2 tsp. light corn syrup**
- **3½ oz. semisweet chocolate,** finely chopped

1. Make the cake Preheat the oven to 350°. Butter a 9-inch round cake pan and line it with parchment paper. In a medium bowl, whisk the flour with the cocoa powder, espresso powder, baking soda and salt. In a large bowl, beat the egg with the sugar and 4 tablespoons of butter until pale, then whisk in both milks and the vanilla. Whisk in the dry ingredients all at once until combined.

2. Scrape the batter into the prepared pan and smooth the top. Bake for 45 to 50 minutes, until a toothpick inserted in the center comes out clean. Let the cake cool completely, about 30 minutes.

3. Make the ganache In a medium saucepan, whisk the cream with the sugar, espresso powder and corn syrup and bring just to a boil. Remove from the heat. Add the chocolate and let stand for 2 minutes, then stir until smooth. Let cool slightly.

4. Invert the cake onto a plate, remove the parchment, then invert it onto a platter. Spread the ganache evenly on top, letting it drip down the side. Let stand until the ganache is set, about 30 minutes. Cut into wedges and serve.

STICKS+ SKEWERS

HASSELBACK YOUR FOOD

To create hassleback (or accordion-style) slices, place a chopstick on either side of a potato or apple half. Cut down until the knife hits the chopsticks. This prevents you from cutting all the way through.

Hasselback Apples with Candied Ginger and Cinnamon

Active **20 min;** Total **1 hr 10 min;** Serves **4**

 4 **Granny Smith apples, halved lengthwise and cored**

 ½ **stick unsalted butter**

 ¼ **cup packed dark brown sugar**

 ¼ **cup minced candied ginger**

 1 **tsp. cinnamon**

 ½ **tsp. kosher salt**

   Vanilla ice cream, for serving

1. Preheat the oven to 375°. Place an apple half cut side down on a work surface and put a chopstick on either side of it. Using a small paring knife, slice the apple crosswise in ⅛-inch intervals, cutting down until the knife hits the chopsticks. Repeat with the remaining apple halves and arrange them peel side up in a large ceramic baking dish.

2. In a small saucepan, melt the butter with the sugar, ginger, cinnamon and salt. Carefully spoon the butter mixture between the slices in the apples, using your fingers to spread them open. Drizzle any remaining butter on top. Cover the baking dish with foil.

3. Bake the apples for about 30 minutes, until nearly tender. Uncover and bake for about 15 minutes longer, until tender and lightly browned. Let cool for 5 minutes, then serve with ice cream.

Hasselback Potatoes with Herb Oil

Active **30 min**; Total **1 hr**; Serves **4**

1½ lbs. fingerling potatoes

1 cup extra-virgin olive oil

   Kosher salt and pepper

1 cup lightly packed basil leaves

¼ cup snipped chives

1 Tbsp. oregano leaves

2 tsp. fresh lemon juice

2 large ice cubes

1. Preheat the oven to 400°. On a work surface, put a chopstick on either side of a potato. Using a small paring knife, slice the potato crosswise in ⅛-inch intervals, cutting down until the knife hits the chopsticks. Repeat with the remaining potatoes.

2. On a large rimmed baking sheet, toss the potatoes with ¼ cup of the olive oil and season with salt and pepper. Roast cut side up for 35 to 40 minutes, until the potatoes are tender and the edges are crisp.

3. Meanwhile, in a blender, pulse the basil with the chives, oregano, lemon juice and ice cubes until the herbs are finely chopped. With the machine on, gradually add the remaining ¾ cup of olive oil until bright green and smooth. Transfer the herb oil to a bowl and season with salt and pepper. Arrange the potatoes on a platter and serve with the herb oil.

MAKE BLOOMING ONIONS

If you're a fan of blooming onions—and, honestly, who isn't?—you can make them yourself with my chopstick hack. The ones served at state fairs are ginormous, but I prefer using smaller Vidalias to maximize the ratio of crisp coating to onion.

 Place a chopstick on either side of the onion root. Slice down the middle of the onion until the knife hits the chopsticks. Continue slicing, rotating the onion between cuts, to form eight even "petals."

Crispy Onion Flowers

Active **30 min**; Total **1 hr**; Serves **6**

- ½ **cup mayonnaise**
- ½ **cup sour cream**
- 2 **Tbsp. minced chives**
- ¾ **tsp. dried oregano**
- ½ **tsp. garlic powder**
- **Kosher salt and pepper**
- **Two 10- to 12-oz. Vidalia onions, peeled, root ends left intact**
- 2 **large eggs**
- ½ **cup whole milk**
- 1½ **cups all-purpose flour**
- 1½ **Tbsp. Old Bay seasoning**
- **Canola oil, for frying**

1. In a medium bowl, whisk the mayonnaise with the sour cream, chives, oregano and garlic powder; season with salt and pepper. Refrigerate the dipping sauce until well chilled, about 15 minutes.

2. Meanwhile, set an onion root side down on a work surface. Place a chopstick on either side of the root. Working carefully with a large, sharp knife, slice down the middle of the onion until the knife hits the chopsticks (this prevents you from cutting all the way through). Continue slicing, rotating the onion between cuts, to make 8 even "petals." Repeat with the remaining onion.

3. In a large bowl, beat the eggs with the milk and a generous pinch of salt. In another large bowl, whisk the flour with the Old Bay and a generous pinch each of salt and pepper.

4. Gently separate the layers of 1 onion and dip it into the egg mixture, turning to coat. Lift the onion out of the mixture, allowing the excess to drip back into the bowl. Dredge the onion in the flour mixture, using a spoon to coat it well, then transfer to a plate. Repeat with the remaining onion. Refrigerate the coated onions for 10 minutes.

5. In a large saucepan, heat 3 inches of oil to 360°. Using a spider or large slotted spoon, carefully lower 1 onion root side down into the hot oil. Fry at 350°, turning occasionally, until golden and crisp, about 4 minutes. Drain on paper towels; season with salt. Repeat with the remaining onion. Transfer the onions to a platter and serve with the dipping sauce.

MAKE AHEAD The sauce can be refrigerated overnight.

SPIRAL-CUT HOT DOGS

What if you could take something that's already delicious and fun like a hot dog and make it even more delicious and fun? My skewer hack to spiralize hot dogs means edges get crisp and hold more toppings–like the three bold ones here. With this trick, you're going to have the coolest-looking hot dogs at your next cookout.

STEP 1 Insert a skewer through each hot dog.

STEP 2 With a small knife, cut at an angle while rolling the hot dog away.

STEP 3 Slide the hot dog off the skewer, then stretch out the spirals.

STEP 4 Grill the hot dogs.

1 Pickled Pepper Slaw

In a bowl, toss 1 cup sliced **sweet and/or hot pickled peppers** with ½ cup shredded **romaine**, ¼ cup each of chopped **parsley** and **dill** and 2 Tbsp. **olive oil**. Season with **salt** and **pepper**; serve on **hot dogs.**

2 Apricot Mostarda

In a saucepan, combine ½ cup each of **apple cider vinegar** and **water** with 1 cup chopped **dried apricots**, 2 Tbsp. **sugar**, 1 minced **shallot** and 1 minced **garlic clove**. Bring to a boil, then simmer over moderate heat, stirring occasionally, until the apricots are soft and coated in a light syrup, 7 to 10 minutes. Stir in 2 Tbsp. **whole-grain mustard** and 1 Tbsp. **Dijon mustard**. Season with **salt** and let cool; serve on **hot dogs**.

3 Chicago-Style Salsa

In a bowl, toss 1 finely chopped **Persian cucumber** with ½ cup **celery leaves**, ½ cup quartered **cherry tomatoes**, ¼ cup thinly sliced **peperoncini**, ¼ cup thinly sliced **red onion**, ¼ cup **sweet pickle relish** and 2 Tbsp. **olive oil**. Season with **salt** and **pepper**; serve on **hot dogs**.

SKEWER A ROAST

You've made a beautiful roast and it's pretty much perfect—until you discover the soggy bottom. That's because when you lay meat right into a pan, the bottom isn't exposed to the hot air in the oven. This skewer hack raises the meat to mimic roasting on a spit so you get a gorgeous crust all over.

Thread two or three skewers through the bottom of a roast. Set the roast over a baking dish so that the skewers raise it above the bottom of the dish.

Beef Rib Roast with Buttermilk Sauce

Active **25 min;** Total **2 hr 20 min**
Serves **4 to 6**

> One 4-lb. beef rib roast (2 or 3 ribs)
>
> Kosher salt and pepper
>
> 2 or 3 long metal skewers

- ½ cup buttermilk
- ¼ cup mayonnaise
- 1 Tbsp. finely chopped tarragon
- 1 tsp. Dijon mustard
- ½ tsp. fresh lemon juice

1. Season the roast generously with salt and pepper and let stand at room temperature for 30 minutes.

2. Preheat the oven to 450°. Set the roast rib side down on a work surface. Thread 2 or 3 skewers through the bottom of the roast. Set the roast over a 9-inch square baking dish so that the skewers hold it above the bottom of the dish. Roast the beef for 30 minutes, until lightly browned. Reduce the oven temperature to 375° and roast for 45 to 55 minutes longer, until an instant-read thermometer inserted in the thickest part of the beef registers 120°.

3. Meanwhile, in a medium bowl, whisk the buttermilk with the mayonnaise, tarragon, mustard and lemon juice. Season with salt and pepper.

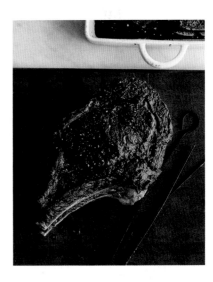

4. Transfer the roast to a cutting board, remove the skewers and let rest for 20 minutes. Carve the roast off the bones and serve, passing the buttermilk sauce at the table.

MAKE AHEAD The buttermilk sauce can be refrigerated overnight.

WAFFLE IRON

COOK EGGS

We've all gotten waffle irons as gifts but somehow never get around to making waffles. The good news is that there are a lot of other ways to use them! I love using mine to cook egg dishes, including okonomiyaki, a Japanese mash-up of an omelet and a pancake.

Waffled Okonomiyaki

📷 OPPOSITE

Total **30 min**; Serves **2**

- 2 **slices of bacon, halved crosswise**
- 2 **large eggs, beaten**
- ½ **cup chicken stock or low-sodium broth**
- 1 **Tbsp. melted butter**
- ½ **cup all-purpose flour**
- ½ **tsp. kosher salt**
- ½ **cup shredded green cabbage**
- ¼ **cup shredded carrot**
- ¼ **cup thinly sliced scallions, plus more for serving**
- **Kewpie mayonnaise (see Note), Sriracha and bonito flakes (optional; see Note), for serving**

 Scatter fillings in the waffle iron and cook without closing. Pour the egg mixture on top and let set. Close the lid without locking to finish cooking.

1. Heat an 8-inch Belgian waffle iron. Add the bacon, close the top and cook on medium-high until browned and crisp, about 5 minutes. Drain on paper towels.

2. In a medium bowl, beat the eggs with the stock, butter, flour and salt. Scatter the cabbage, carrot and ¼ cup of scallions on the waffle iron and cook on high, without closing, until sizzling, about 30 seconds. Gradually pour the egg mixture on top and cook, without closing, until the eggs just start to set on the bottom, 20 to 30 seconds. Close the top without locking it and cook until the eggs are set, 30 seconds to 1 minute longer.

3. Open the iron and, using a spatula, fold the okonomiyaki in half; transfer to a plate. Serve topped with the bacon, Kewpie, Sriracha, bonito and sliced scallions.

NOTE Look for Kewpie mayonnaise (which is made with rice vinegar, and very popular in Japan) and bonito flakes at Asian markets.

Waffled Denver Omelet

Total **30 min**; Serves **4**

- **Nonstick cooking spray**
- 8 **large eggs**
- **Kosher salt and pepper**
- ½ **cup finely chopped baked ham**
- ½ **cup very thinly sliced red onion**
- ¼ **cup finely chopped green bell pepper**
- ¾ **cup shredded cheddar cheese, plus more for serving**
- **Finely chopped parsley, for garnish**

1. Heat an 8-inch Belgian waffle iron and coat with nonstick spray. In a medium bowl, beat the eggs with a generous pinch each of salt and pepper.

2. Scatter one-fourth of the ham, onion and bell pepper on the waffle iron and cook on high, without closing, until sizzling, about 30 seconds. Gradually pour one-fourth of the beaten eggs on top and cook, without closing, until the eggs just start to set on the bottom, 20 to 30 seconds. Close the iron without locking it (to allow the batter to expand) and cook until the eggs are set, 30 seconds to 1 minute longer.

3. Open the iron and scatter one-fourth of the cheese over the omelet. Using a spatula, fold the omelet in half and transfer to a plate. Top with more cheese and chopped parsley and serve. Repeat with the remaining ingredients to form 3 more omelets, spraying the waffle iron between batches.

MAKE POTATO WAFFLES

You can give potato pancakes a serious upgrade by waffling them. You'll get all these awesome crisp nooks and crannies and the center will still be deliciously soft. Plus, you won't even have to flip the waffles because the iron cooks them on both sides.

STEP 1 In a large bowl, stir together all of the ingredients for the potato waffles.

STEP 2 AND 3 Spread the mixture onto a buttered preheated waffle iron. Close and let cook until the waffle is golden and crisp.

Waffled Potato Blini with Smoked Salmon

Total **40 min**; Serves **4**

- 2 lbs. baking potatoes—peeled, coarsely shredded and squeezed dry
- 1 medium onion, shredded
- 2 large eggs, lightly beaten
- 3 Tbsp. all-purpose flour
- 1½ tsp. kosher salt
- 1 tsp. baking powder
- 2 Tbsp. chopped dill, plus more for garnish
- 3 Tbsp. melted unsalted butter, plus more for brushing

  Smoked salmon and sour cream, for serving

1. Heat an 8-inch standard waffle iron and preheat the oven to 200°. In a large bowl, mix the potatoes with the onion, eggs, flour, salt, baking powder, the 2 tablespoons of dill and 3 tablespoons of butter.

2. Brush the waffle iron with melted butter and spread one-fourth of the potato mixture onto it. Close and cook on high until the blini is golden and crisp, 5 to 7 minutes. Transfer to a rack in the oven to keep warm. Repeat with the remaining potato mixture to make 3 more blini. Serve the blini topped with smoked salmon, sour cream and dill.

NOTE These blini can also be made in a Belgian waffle maker to serve 3: Spoon one-third of the mixture onto the waffle iron instead of one-fourth.

CONTINUED ▶

POTATO WAFFLES
3 MORE WAYS

Once I mastered potato pancakes in the waffle iron, I created variations based on my favorite foods, like kimchi pancakes and loaded baked potatoes. I even made a dessert version with sweet potatoes. If you're cooking in batches, transfer the waffles directly to a rack in a 200° oven. (You don't want to lose any of the crispness!) The recipes here each serve four.

1 Potato, Kimchi and Scallion Waffles

Peel, coarsely shred and squeeze dry 2 lbs. **baking potatoes.** Mix in a bowl with 1 cup thinly sliced drained **kimchi,** 1 cup julienned **scallions,** 2 **large eggs,** ¼ cup **flour,** 3 Tbsp. melted **unsalted butter,** 1 tsp. **kosher salt** and 1 tsp. **baking powder.** Brush a heated 8-inch standard waffle iron with melted **butter** and spread one-fourth of the potato mixture on it. Close and cook on high until golden, 7 to 9 minutes. Keep warm. Repeat with the remaining potato mixture. In a bowl, whisk 3 Tbsp. **low-sodium soy sauce,** 1 Tbsp. **rice vinegar,** 1 tsp. **toasted sesame seeds** and ½ tsp. **toasted sesame oil.** Garnish the waffles with julienned **scallions** and **sesame seeds** and serve with the sauce.

2 Loaded Potato Waffles

Peel, coarsely shred and squeeze dry 2 lbs. **baking potatoes**. Mix in a bowl with ¾ cup shredded **extra-sharp cheddar cheese**, 2 large **eggs**, 3 Tbsp. **all-purpose flour**, 3 Tbsp. melted **unsalted butter**, 1½ tsp. **kosher salt** and 1 tsp. **baking powder**. Fold in ½ cup crumbled **cooked bacon** and ⅓ cup chopped **chives**. Brush a heated 8-inch standard waffle iron with melted **butter** and spread one-fourth of the potato mixture on it. Close and cook on high until the waffle is golden and crisp, 5 to 7 minutes. Keep warm. Repeat with the remaining potato mixture. Serve topped with **sour cream**, crumbled **bacon**, shredded **cheddar** and chopped **chives**.

3 Sweet Potato Waffles with Fluff

Peel, coarsely shred and squeeze dry 2 lbs. **sweet potatoes**. Mix in a bowl with 2 large **eggs**, ¼ cup **all-purpose flour**, 3 Tbsp. melted **unsalted butter**, 2 Tbsp. **light brown sugar**, 1½ tsp. **cinnamon**, 1 tsp. **baking powder** and ¾ tsp. **kosher salt**. Brush a heated 8-inch standard waffle iron with melted **butter** and spread one-fourth of the potato mixture on it. Close and cook on high until the waffle is golden and crisp, 5 to 7 minutes. Keep warm. Repeat with the remaining potato mixture. Serve topped with **Marshmallow Fluff** and chopped **toasted pecans**.

PRESS SANDWICHES

If you own a waffle iron, you don't ever need to buy a panini press—sorry, panini press makers! Just load your sandwich into your waffle iron and shut the lid. You'll get a piping-hot grilled sandwich with extra-crisp bread and gooey cheese that stretches for yards.

Waffled Muffuletta

📷 OPPOSITE

Total **30 min;** Serves **4**

- 4 **soft ciabatta or kaiser rolls, split and hollowed out**
- 1⅓ **cups shredded provolone cheese**
- ½ **cup sliced pitted green olives**
- ¼ **cup extra-virgin olive oil, plus more for brushing**
- 2 **Tbsp. plus 2 tsp. red wine vinegar**

  Kosher salt and pepper
- 16 **thin slices of mortadella**
- ¼ **cup chopped jarred hot cherry peppers**

 Add a sandwich to the waffle iron and close the top without locking it. Let cook, pressing down gently on the lid occasionally, until the sandwich is crunchy on the outside and the cheese is melted.

1. Open the rolls on a work surface. On the bottom half of each roll, spoon ⅓ cup of cheese and 2 tablespoons of olives. Drizzle each with 1 tablespoon of olive oil and 2 teaspoons of red wine vinegar and season with salt and pepper. Top with the mortadella. Spread the chopped hot cherry peppers evenly on the roll tops and close the sandwiches, pressing to flatten them.

2. Heat an 8-inch Belgian waffle iron. Brush both sides of a sandwich with olive oil, add to the waffle iron and close the top without locking it. Cook on high, pressing down gently on the waffle iron occasionally, until the sandwich is crispy on the outside and the cheese is melted, 4 to 5 minutes. Repeat with the remaining sandwiches.

Waffled Croissants with Prosciutto

Total **30 min;** Serves **4**

A croissant makes the ultimate grilled sandwich. It's so buttery it's almost like a self-basting bread in the waffle iron.

- 4 **croissants, split**
- 4 **oz. thinly sliced prosciutto**
- 2 **cups arugula (not baby), thick stems discarded**
- 1½ **oz. Asiago cheese, shredded (1⅓ cups)**

1. Heat an 8-inch Belgian waffle iron. Open the croissants on a work surface and pile the prosciutto, arugula and cheese on the bottoms. Close the sandwiches, pressing to flatten them.

2. Add a sandwich to the waffle iron and close the top without locking it. Cook on medium, pressing down gently on the waffle iron occasionally, until the sandwich is crispy on the outside and the cheese is melted, 4 to 5 minutes. Repeat with the remaining sandwiches.

GRIDDLE DESSERTS

 Add batter or dough to a heated waffle iron. Close the lid for no-bake desserts.

Waffled Brownie Sundaes

Total **30 min**; Makes **2 large waffles**

- 2 oz. semisweet chocolate, finely chopped
- 6 Tbsp. unsalted butter, softened, plus melted butter for brushing
- ½ cup sugar
- 2 large eggs
- 1 tsp. pure vanilla extract
- ½ cup plus 2 Tbsp. all-purpose flour
- ¼ cup unsweetened cocoa powder
- ½ tsp. baking powder
- ½ tsp. kosher salt
- Vanilla ice cream and sprinkles, for serving

1. In a large microwave-safe bowl, melt the chopped chocolate in the 6 tablespoons of butter in 20-second intervals; whisk until smooth. Whisk in the sugar, eggs and vanilla until smooth, then whisk in the flour, cocoa powder, baking powder and salt.

2. Heat an 8-inch Belgian waffle iron and brush it lightly with melted butter. Add half of the brownie batter, close the lid and cook on medium until the waffle is crisp on the outside and cooked through, 4 to 5 minutes. Repeat with the remaining batter. Serve the waffles with vanilla ice cream and sprinkles.

Cinnamon-Cardamom Bun Waffles

📷 OPPOSITE

Active **1 hr**; Total **3 hr 30 min**; Makes **6 large waffles or 24 individual buns**

DOUGH

- ¾ cup whole milk
- ½ cup granulated sugar
- 1 Tbsp. active dry yeast
- 2 large eggs
- 6 Tbsp. unsalted butter, softened, plus more for brushing
- 1 tsp. finely grated lemon zest
- ½ tsp. kosher salt
- 3½ cups all-purpose flour
- ½ cup packed light brown sugar
- 2 tsp. cinnamon
- 1 tsp. ground cardamom

ICING

- 1¼ cups confectioners' sugar
- 4 Tbsp. unsalted butter, melted
- 3 Tbsp. whole milk
- Pearled sugar, for sprinkling

1. Make the dough In a microwave-safe glass, heat the milk until barely warm. Pour into a stand mixer fitted with the dough hook and stir in the granulated sugar and yeast. Let stand until the yeast is foamy, about 5 minutes. Add the eggs, 6 tablespoons of butter, the lemon zest and salt, then add the flour and beat at medium speed until a soft dough forms, about 3 minutes. Increase the speed to medium-high and beat until the dough is soft and supple, about 5 minutes longer.

2. Scrape the dough out onto a lightly floured surface, form it into a ball and transfer to a lightly buttered bowl. Cover with plastic wrap and let stand in a warm place until doubled in bulk, 1 to 2 hours.

3. Line a baking sheet with parchment paper and butter the paper. Turn the dough out onto a lightly floured surface and roll it out to a 15-by-20-inch rectangle. In a small bowl, mix the brown sugar with the cinnamon and cardamom. Sprinkle the sugar mixture evenly over the dough.

4. Tightly roll up the dough to form a 24- to 26-inch-long log (it will stretch as you roll it). Working quickly, trim the ends of the log, then cut the log into 24 rounds. Arrange the rounds cut side up on the prepared baking sheet, cover lightly with plastic and let rise in a warm place until puffy, about 1 hour.

5. Heat an 8-inch Belgian waffle iron and brush it lightly with butter. Add 4 buns cut side up, close the top and cook until the buns are golden on the outside and cooked through, 3 to 5 minutes. Transfer to a rack. Repeat with the remaining buns.

6. Make the icing In a medium bowl, whisk the confectioners' sugar with the butter and milk until thick. Drizzle the buns with the glaze and sprinkle with pearled sugar. If the buns stick together, tear them apart before serving.

MAKE AHEAD The buns can be made up to 2 hours ahead. Warm in a 225° oven before glazing and serving.

WINE BOTTLE

PIT CHERRIES

Who owns a cherry pitter? I don't, and you don't need to invest in one either. For my cherry-pitting hack, all you need is an empty wine bottle (we've all got those) and a chopstick. Get excited for all the cherry pies you can make!

 Rest a cherry, stem side up, on the opening of an empty wine bottle. Using the thick end of a chopstick, push the pit into the bottle.

Bibb Salad with Fennel, Cherries and Walnuts

Total **40 min;** Serves **4 to 6**

 1 cup walnuts
2½ Tbsp. sherry vinegar
 2 Tbsp. minced shallots
 1 Tbsp. Dijon mustard
 ¼ cup extra-virgin olive oil
    Kosher salt and pepper
    Two 5-oz. heads of Bibb lettuce, cored and leaves torn
 1 medium fennel bulb—halved, cored and very thinly sliced
1½ lbs. fresh sweet cherries, pitted and halved or quartered
 ¼ cup snipped fennel fronds

1. Preheat the oven to 375°. Spread the walnuts in a pie plate and toast for about 8 minutes, until golden. Let cool, then coarsely chop.

2. Meanwhile, in a large serving bowl, whisk the sherry vinegar with the shallots; let stand for 5 minutes. Whisk in the mustard and olive oil until incorporated, then season with salt and pepper. Add the lettuce and fennel and toss well. Add the walnuts, cherries and fennel fronds, season with salt and pepper and toss again. Serve right away.

how to use cherry pits

INFUSED VODKA After you've collected a bunch of cherry pits in a wine bottle, add vodka along with a few whole cherries. Let infuse for at least one week. You can use the cherry vodka in my Mixed-Berry Martini on page 132.

CHERRY SELTZER Add sparkling water to some cherry pits in a wine bottle. Swirl, then strain into ice-filled glasses.

POUND MEAT

 Place meat on a large piece of plastic wrap. Drizzle with a little water and spread out another piece of plastic on top. Holding a wine bottle by the neck, lightly pound the meat.

Spicy Chicken Milanese
Total **15 min**; Serves **2**

- 2 large eggs
- 3 Tbsp. Dijon mustard
- 1½ tsp. cayenne pepper
  Kosher salt and black pepper
- 1½ cups panko
  Two 6-oz. chicken breast cutlets, lightly pounded ¼ inch thick
- ⅓ cup plus 1 Tbsp. olive oil
- 2 cups grape tomatoes, halved
- 1 Tbsp. fresh lemon juice
- ¼ cup chopped parsley
  Freshly shaved Parmigiano-Reggiano cheese

1. In a pie plate, beat the eggs with the mustard and cayenne; season with salt and black pepper. Spread the panko in another pie plate. Dip the chicken in the egg mixture, then dredge in the panko; press to help it adhere.

2. In a large skillet, heat ⅓ cup of the oil until shimmering. Cook the chicken over moderately high heat, turning once, until browned outside and white throughout, 4 to 6 minutes. Transfer to plates.

3. Meanwhile, in a medium bowl, toss the tomatoes, lemon juice and parsley with the remaining 1 tablespoon of olive oil; season with salt and pepper. Spoon the tomatoes over the chicken and garnish with cheese. Serve immediately.

Pounded Beef Tenderloin with Hearts of Palm Salad

Total **30 min**; Serves **4**

- 1 lb. center-cut beef tenderloin, cut crosswise into 4 slices and lightly pounded ⅛ inch thick
- 2 Tbsp. extra-virgin olive oil, plus more for brushing

  Kosher salt and pepper
- 1½ Tbsp. fresh lemon juice, plus lemon wedges for serving
- 2 Tbsp. minced shallot
- 1½ tsp. Dijon mustard
- 4 oz. watercress, thick stems discarded (6 cups)

  One 15-oz. can hearts of palm, drained and sliced ¼ inch thick on the diagonal
- 1 Hass avocado, peeled and cut into 1-inch pieces
- ⅓ cup snipped chives

1. Heat a large grill pan for 10 minutes. Brush the steaks with oil; season with salt and pepper. Grill over high heat until lightly charred, 45 seconds. Flip the steaks and grill until medium-rare, 30 seconds. Transfer to plates.

2. In a large bowl, whisk the 2 tablespoons of oil with the lemon juice, shallot and mustard; season with salt and pepper. Add the watercress, hearts of palm and avocado, season with salt and pepper and toss. Mound the salad beside the steaks, top with the chives and serve with lemon wedges.

WINE BOTTLE

ROLL OUT BREAD WRAPPERS

By rolling squishy white bread really thin, you can make wrappers for three kinds of fried hors d'oeuvres. Big thanks to Andrew Zimmern, host of Travel Channel's *Bizarre Foods*, for this tip!

STEP 1 Cut the crusts off sliced white bread.

STEP 2 Roll each slice until extremely thin.

STEP 3 Spoon filling into each bread wrapper and seal with water.

Asian Shrimp Rolls

📷 PAGE 243

Total **45 min**; Makes **14**

- 2 Tbsp. canola oil, plus more for frying
- ½ cup minced cabbage
- ¼ cup minced carrot
- 1 Tbsp. finely grated peeled fresh ginger
- ¾ lb. shelled and deveined shrimp, minced
- 4 scallions, finely chopped, plus slices for garnish
- 2 Tbsp. unseasoned rice vinegar
- 2 tsp. cornstarch
- ½ tsp. toasted sesame oil
  Kosher salt and pepper
- 1 large egg, beaten
- 14 slices of white sandwich bread, crusts removed
  Sambal oelek and Kewpie mayonnaise (see Note on p. 225), for serving

1. In a large skillet, heat the 2 tablespoons of oil. Add the cabbage, carrot and ginger and cook over moderate heat, stirring occasionally, until softened, 3 to 5 minutes. Add the shrimp and cook until just white throughout, about 3 minutes. Stir in the chopped scallions, rice vinegar, cornstarch and sesame oil and cook for 1 minute. Scrape into a medium bowl and let cool. Season the filling with salt and pepper, then mix in the egg. Refrigerate for 15 minutes.

2. Using a rolling pin or wine bottle, flatten each slice of bread; arrange with the long sides facing you. Spoon 1 heaping tablespoon of the filling on the lower half of each slice. Brush the edges with water and roll up the bread around the filling; press the seams and open ends to seal the rolls.

3. In a large, deep skillet, heat 1 inch of oil to 350°. Fry the rolls in batches, turning occasionally, until crisp, about 2 minutes per batch. Transfer the shrimp rolls to paper towels to drain. Sprinkle with sliced scallions and serve with sambal oelek and Kewpie mayonnaise.

CONTINUED ▶

► CONTINUED

ROLL OUT BREAD WRAPPERS

Crispy Cheese Sticks

📷 PAGE 241

Total **45 min;** Makes **14**

1½ cups shredded mozzarella

½ cup freshly grated Parmigiano-
Reggiano cheese

1 large egg, beaten

2 Tbsp. minced parsley

½ tsp. crushed red pepper

Kosher salt and black pepper

14 slices of white sandwich bread,
crusts removed

Canola oil, for frying

Warm marinara sauce, for serving

1. In a medium bowl, mix both cheeses
with the egg, parsley, crushed red pepper and ½ teaspoon each of salt and
black pepper; refrigerate for 15 minutes.

2. Using a rolling pin or wine bottle, flatten each slice of bread; arrange with the
long sides facing you. Spoon 1 heaping
tablespoon of the cheese filling on the
lower half of each slice. Brush the edges
with water and roll up the bread around
the filling; press the seams and open
ends to seal the rolls.

3. In a large, deep skillet, heat 1 inch of oil
to 350°. Fry the rolls in batches, turning
occasionally, until crisp, about 2 minutes
per batch. Drain on paper towels, sprinkle
with salt and serve with marinara.

Cuban Picadillo Rolls

Total **45 min;** Makes **14**

2 Tbsp. canola oil, plus more
for frying

½ cup minced onion

½ cup minced red bell pepper

3 garlic cloves, minced

2 tsp. cumin seeds

½ lb. lean ground sirloin

¼ cup minced pimiento-stuffed
green olives

¼ cup golden raisins, soaked in hot
water for 5 minutes and drained

2 Tbsp. tomato paste

Kosher salt and pepper

1 large egg, beaten

14 slices of white sandwich bread,
crusts removed

Lime wedges and hot sauce,
for serving

1. In a large skillet, heat the 2 tablespoons
of oil. Add the onion, bell pepper, garlic
and cumin and cook over moderately high
heat, stirring occasionally, until softened
and just starting to brown, 5 minutes.
Add the sirloin and cook, breaking up the
meat, until just cooked through, 5 to
7 minutes. Stir in the olives, raisins and
tomato paste until combined. Scrape into
a bowl and let cool. Season generously
with salt and pepper, then mix in the egg.
Refrigerate the filling for 15 minutes.

2. Using a rolling pin or wine bottle, flatten each slice of bread; arrange with
the long sides facing you. Spoon 1 heaping tablespoon of the filling on the lower
half of each slice. Brush the edges with
water and roll up the bread around the
filling; press the seams and open ends
to seal the rolls.

3. In a large, deep skillet, heat 1 inch of oil
to 350°. Fry the rolls in batches, turning
occasionally, until crisp, about 2 minutes
per batch. Drain the picadillo rolls on
paper towels, sprinkle with salt and serve
with lime wedges and hot sauce.

MAKE AHEAD The picadillo filling can be
refrigerated overnight.

CRUSH SEEDS AND PEPPERCORNS

A wine bottle is just the right weight for pulverizing lots of seeds or peppercorns at once. The grooves at the bottom of the glass help, too. Just make sure to use a clean bottle!

 Place seeds (or peppercorns) in a large resealable plastic bag. Holding a wine bottle by the neck, set it in the bag and lightly pound the seeds until crushed.

Pepita-Crusted Chicken Cutlets

Total **45 min**; Serves **4**

- 1½ **cups pepitas (hulled pumpkin seeds)**
- 1 **tsp. ancho chile powder**
- ½ **tsp. ground cumin**
- **Pinch of cayenne pepper**
- **Kosher salt and black pepper**
- ¾ **cup all-purpose flour**
- 2 **large eggs**
- **Four 4-oz. chicken cutlets**
- **Canola oil, for frying**
- **Cilantro sprigs, lime wedges and sour cream, for serving**

1. Preheat the oven to 375°. Spread the pepitas on a large rimmed baking sheet and bake for 5 to 7 minutes, until very lightly browned. Let cool, then transfer to a large resealable plastic bag. Hold the bag upright and set the bottom of a clean wine bottle in it. Holding the neck of the bottle, lightly pound the pepitas with the bottom of the bottle until they're finely crushed. Mix in the chile powder, cumin, cayenne, ½ teaspoon of salt and ¼ teaspoon of black pepper.

2. Spread the flour in a shallow bowl. In another shallow bowl, beat the eggs. Season the chicken cutlets with salt and black pepper and dredge them in the flour, shaking off any excess. Dip the cutlets in the eggs, then coat thoroughly with the crushed pepitas, pressing to help them adhere.

3. In a large skillet, heat ¼ inch of canola oil until shimmering. Add half of the chicken and cook over moderate heat, turning once, until golden and crispy, about 3 minutes per side. Transfer the chicken to a large baking sheet. Repeat with the remaining chicken. Transfer the baking sheet to the oven and bake for about 7 minutes, until an instant-read thermometer inserted in the thickest piece registers 160°. Serve the chicken with cilantro sprigs, lime wedges and sour cream.

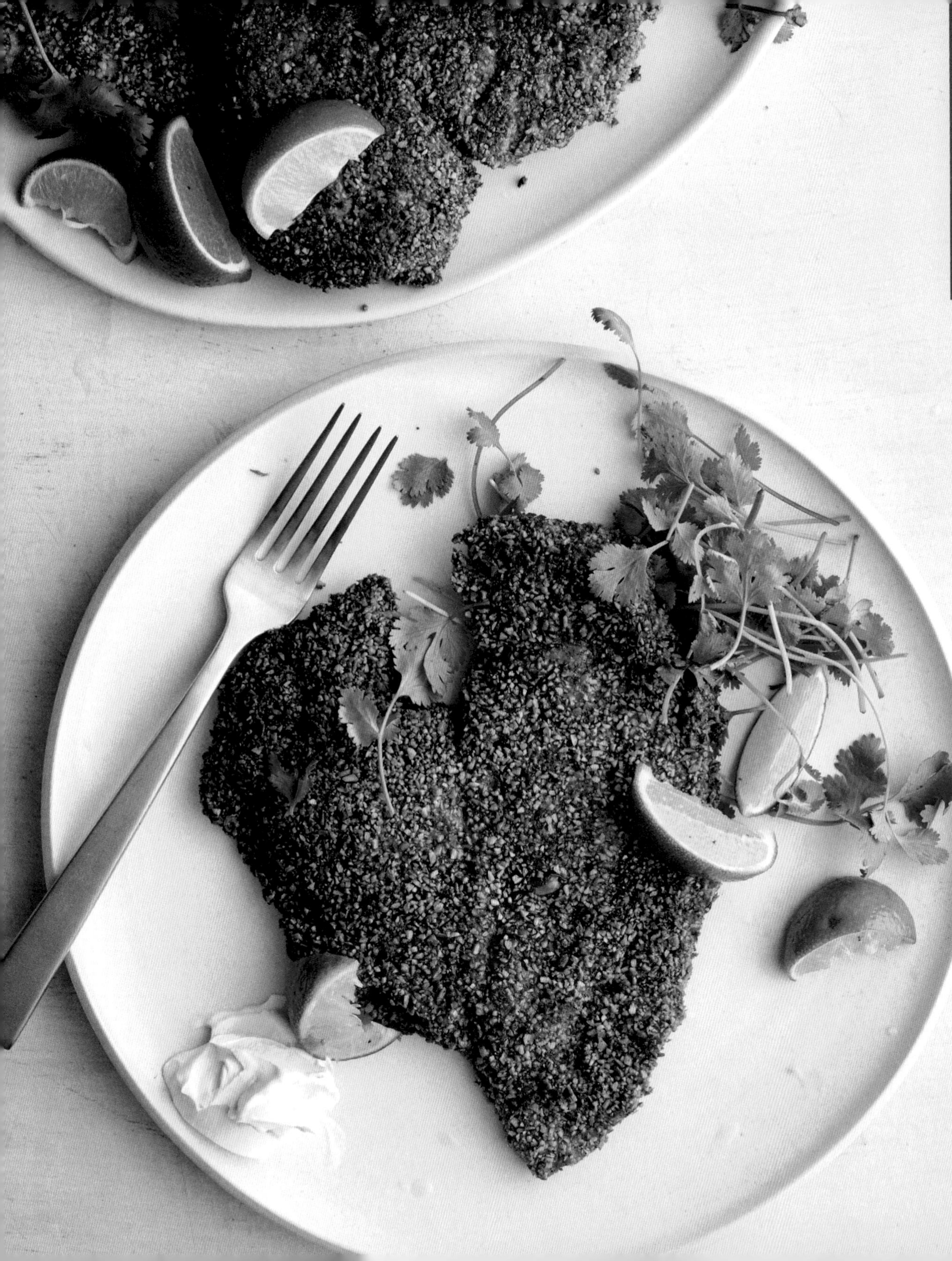

INDEX

HERB AND BULGUR
SALAD WITH SUNFLOWER
SEEDS, P. 207

R

S

BRUSSELS SPROUT
AND ROBIOLA
PIZZA WITH FRESH
TOMATO SAUCE,
P. 32

photo contributors

NICOLE FRANZEN 46, 47, 62, 63, 64, 120, 121, 122, 123, 151, 152, 153, 198, 209, 218, 219

CHRISTINA HOLMES 10 (bacon), 24, 25, 105 (meatballs), 118, 119, 142, 172, 173, 174, 175, 187, 256

JOHN KERNICK 4, 9, 10 (all except bacon), 12, 14, 15, 16, 18, 19, 20, 22, 26, 27, 28, 29, 30, 32, 33, 34, 36, 37, 38, 40, 41, 42, 44, 45, 48, 49, 50, 51, 52, 53, 54–55, 56, 57, 58, 60, 66, 67, 68, 70, 72, 74, 75, 76, 78, 79, 80, 83, 84, 86, 87, 88, 89, 90, 92, 94, 95 (all except bottom right), 97, 100, 104, 105 (ginger), 106, 107, 108, 109, 110, 112, 113, 114, 115, 117, 124, 126, 128, 129, 130, 133, 134, 137, 138, 139, 140, 141, 145, 146, 149, 150, 154, 155, 157, 158, 159, 160, 162, 164, 165, 169, 170, 176, 177, 178, 179, 180, 181, 183, 184, 185, 186, 188, 189, 190, 192, 193, 194, 196, 197, 201, 202, 204, 205, 206, 207, 210, 211, 212, 214, 215, 216, 220, 221, 222, 224, 226, 227, 228–229, 230, 233, 234, 237, 238, 240, 241, 242, 243, 245, 246–247, 251, 254

EVA KOLENKO 95 (bottom right), 102, 166

CON POULOS 98, 132, 239

MORE BOOKS FROM FOOD & WINE

STAFF FAVORITES The editors of FOOD & WINE share over 150 of their most cherished recipes: fast starters, make-ahead main courses, outrageous desserts and more.

F&W ANNUAL COOKBOOK More than 680 recipes—all tested and perfected in the F&W kitchen—from legends like Alice Waters and Jacques Pépin and star chefs like Mario Batali, Carla Hall and Tyler Florence.

MARKET MATH Based on FOOD & WINE magazine's popular Market Math column, this book transforms 50 everyday ingredients into 200 fast, fresh and delicious weeknight meals.

TO ORDER, CALL 800-284-4145 OR VISIT **FOODANDWINE.COM/BOOKS**